# Land Entries
## *of*
# Hyde County
# North Carolina
## *- 1778-1795 -*

*Compiled by:*
*Dr. A.B. Pruitt*

**Southern Historical Press, Inc.**
**Greenville, South Carolina**

This volume was reproduced
from a personal copy located in
the Publishers private library

Please direct all correspondence and book orders to:
**www.southernhistoricalpress.com**
**or**
**SOUTHERN HISTORICAL PRESS, Inc.**
**1071 Park West Blvd.**
**Greenville, SC    29611**

**Southernhistoricalpress@gmail.com**

# Introduction

This book contains abstracts of land entries in Hyde County, North Carolina. The entries in this book are found in the North Carolina Archives in books SS 955.3 (Nos. 1-454) and SS 955.4 (Nos. 455-942). This material isn't on microfilm.

Hyde County was formed about 1712 by changing the name of Wickham County to Craven County. Dare County was formed from part of Hyde County in 1870. Part of Currituck County was attached to Hyde County in 1745 and 1823; part of Carteret County was attached to Hyde County in 1845; part of Hyde County was attached to Beaufort County in 1819. Among the early records of Hyde County which have been published are: Hyde County cemeteries by Martha R Swindell & R. S. Spencer jr, 1910 census by Hyde County Historial Society, and Hyde Remembers (Bible records) by R. S. Spencer jr. Also there is the High Tides, the journal of the Hyde County Historical Society.

An earlier land grant in 1723 is mentioned in this book in entry 529. A grant to the Indians is mentioned in entries 224. 251, 285. Metes an bounds are given in the following entries: 6, 15, 18, 24, 31, 68, 73, 142, 212, and 336.

Land speculators were active throughout North Carolina and the other states in the 1790s. Sometimes the speculators hired an agent to make the entry, but the speculator received the grant. It was common in North Carolina for speculators to make several entries for 640 acres each because the fees per acre increased for larger entries. The speculators then grouped several 640 acre entries into one large survey and grant. The speculators hoped to divide the large tracts into smaller tracts and sell the tracts, for a profit, to new settlers or to out-of-state investors. This speculation was halted or interrupted by a financial panic in the late 1790s and because the speculators couldn't pay the taxes on the land. Some of this land was escheated (sold back to) the State and regranted. Major speculators in Hyde County were Richard Blackledge and John Gray Blount. Some of the entries numbered 705 to 904 in this book were used by Blount to get a grant for 100,000 ac composing most of present day Dare County. Blount also obtained, from John Hall, a grant for 190,840 ac in Hyde County.

An entry is a claim made to the appointed entry taker by the enterer for vacant or unclaimed land that was technically the property of the State. The enterer described the land--number of acres, nearby waterways, and neighboring land holders. If there were no problems, the entry taker issued a warrant to the county surveyor to survey the land. The warrant and survey may also describe the land and give additional land marks not mentioned in the original entry. The warrant and completed survey were sent to the Secretary of State. A grant or patent was then issued, and the person receiving the grant usually had about twelve months to register the grant in the county.

However, problems or counter claims did often appear. Some of these problems were:

(1) A "caveat" could be issued (after the entry and before the grant) to stop the grant from being issued. The person making a caveat could say he already owned part or all of the land. The entry taker usually indicated in the entry book if a caveat was made against all or part of an entry an entry and who made the caveat. Then a jury would settle the dispute. This decision could be: (a) in favor of the caveater in which case the entry was void or discontinued or the enterer withdrew the entry and the caveater did nothing more; or (b) in favor of the caveater for part of the entry and the caveater retained his part of the land and the enterer obtained a grant for the remainder; or (c) in favor of the caveater and the caveater made a later entry on the land and obtained a grant; or (d) in favor of the enterer so he gets a grant for the land.

(2) After the entry was made and the warrant issued, the surveyor may encounter problems finding enough vacant land. This problem was usually resolved by changing the entry so the number of acres matched the survey. The entry taker often made corrections in the entry book in the case of shortages by writing the new number on top of the original entry.

(3) Fees were required to cover the entry, warrant, survey, & grant. If any fee was not paid, the entry was usually discontinued or abandoned and the land was still "vacant" for someone to claim. This later claim may be (a) by a later numbered entry or (b) by using the same entry number and the entry taker wrote the new name on top of the original name.

(4) In addition to the above problems, the entry taker may have made normal mistakes while writing in the entry book. So some "write overs" indicated in my abstracts may be due to entry taker's error and some may be due to problems encountered during the process of obtaining the grant.

Prior to 1777 obtaining land in North Carolina was done through the Council of State or Court of Claims. Records of land grants survive in the Secretary of State's Office; some of the land entries for these grants are in the Archives. In 1777, a new law reorganized the land entry system in North Carolina as the State took over granting land from the Crown and Granville's agents. Under this law one entry taker was to be appointed in each county. It was under this law that the land entries in this book were made. In 1795 the entry law was revised. Part of that revision required the clerks of the county courts to collect and copy all the entry taker's books for each county. The transcripts were forwarded to the Secretary of State. The transcript for Hyde County is in SS 955.3 and 955.4.

In my abstracts, I have tried to adhere to the following format:

(a) Entry number or a sequential number (for indexing purposes) followed by the entry number given in the book.

(b) Date of the entry.

(c) Name of person making the entry or claim; number of acres; and description of the land (usually) in this order: waterways, neighboring land owners (following the word "border"), roads, etc, and an indication if any "improvement" was mentioned.

Often in the entry book extra information about the entry is written in the margin. I have put this marginal information at the end of the entry. The punctuation is almost entirely mine and is included to aid the reader and divide the parts of entry into the areas described above. Please note: "granted" usually means the warrant of survey was issued, not that a grant was issued for a particular entry.

If you find an "interesting" land entry, please write the Land Office (part of the Secretary of State's Office); in the future these records will be microfilmed and moved to the Archives. Give the person's name and county because that's how the information is filed there. If the grant was completed, there will probably (but not always) be a copy of the warrant for survey and the survey in the Land Office. The warrant often gives information quite similar to the land entry. The survey is more valuable in locating the land and usually includes a plat giving compass directions and distances between the corners. The chain bearers are often mentioned on the survey but neighboring land holders aren't mentioned as often. Using the entry, warrant, & survey, it is much easier to find the land and determine you have the correct grant when the number of acres changes after the original entry.

If you know a person owned land in Hyde County, do not despair if you don't find an entry for him in this book. Many entries were made prior to 1777. Some of these entries survive as noted above. Also the warrant and/or survey may exist in the Land Office (currently in the Secretary of State's Office; in the Archives in the future). Or, the grant may survive in the Land Office or county deeds. So, the entry may be lost, but the grant might still exist. When writing the Land Office, send the person's name and county or counties where he lived because that's how the information is filed.

Please refer to <u>North Carolina Research Genealogy and Local History</u> by H. F. M. Leary and M. R. Stirewalt for additional information about land entries and the land granting process in North Carolina. This book also contains a dictionary of legal terms often encountered in genealogical work as well as almost everything a genealogist needs to know about North Carolina research.

A map in this book is included to help the reader locate the creeks which are mentioned most often in the index. The creek locations are not meant to be exact. More complete and accurate maps of the counties can be obtained from the North Carolina Department of Transportation or in a book of maps for all North Carolina counties from County Maps (Puetz place, Lyndon Station, WI). Also the North Carolina Archives sells a set of maps including maps of the state for 1775, 1808, and 1833. The state Water Resources Department has produced a set of maps showing creeks and rivers.

An index has been provided for this book.  The numbers in the index are the entry numbers, not the page numbers.  At the end of the index is a section devoted to geographical place names, i.e. creek, rivers, fords, forks, etc.

The author wishes to thank the North Carolina Archives for preserving these entry books and thank the staff for their courteous retrieval of the books from the stacks.  He would also like to thank the people who brought forth affordable computers, printers, and software without which the preparation of this book would have been much more arduous.

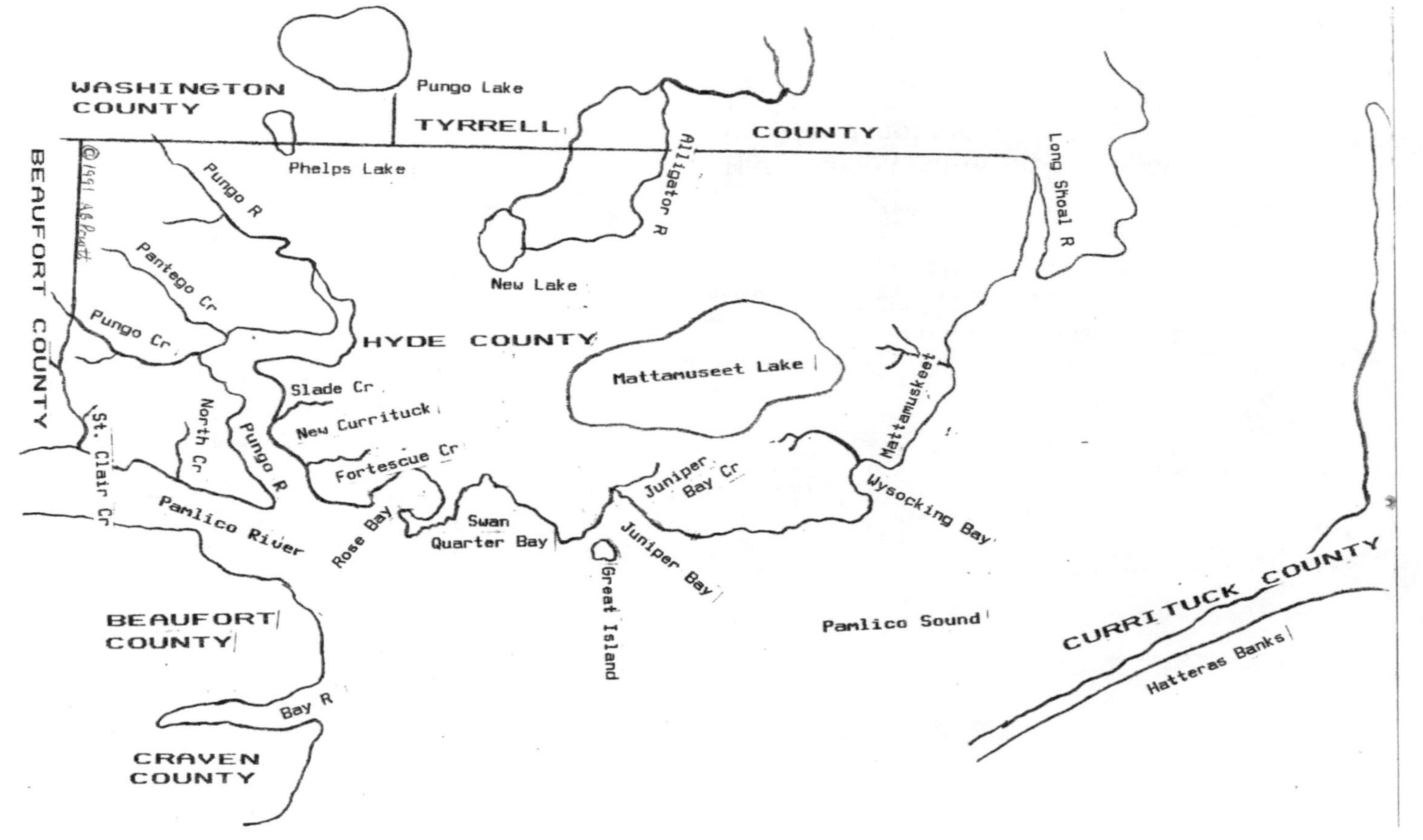

WASHINGTON COUNTY
Pungo Lake
TYRRELL          COUNTY
BEAUFORT COUNTY
© 1991 AB Pruitt
Pungo R
Phelps Lake
Alligator R
Long Shoal R
Pantego Cr
Pungo Cr
New Lake
HYDE COUNTY
Mattamuseet Lake
Mattamuskeet
Slade Cr
North Cr
Pungo R
New Currituck
Fortescue Cr
Juniper Bay Cr
Wysocking Bay
St. Clair Cr
Pamlico River
Rose Bay
Swan Quarter Bay
Juniper Bay
Great Island
Pamlico Sound
CURRITUCK COUNTY
BEAUFORT COUNTY
Bay R
Hatteras Banks
CRAVEN COUNTY

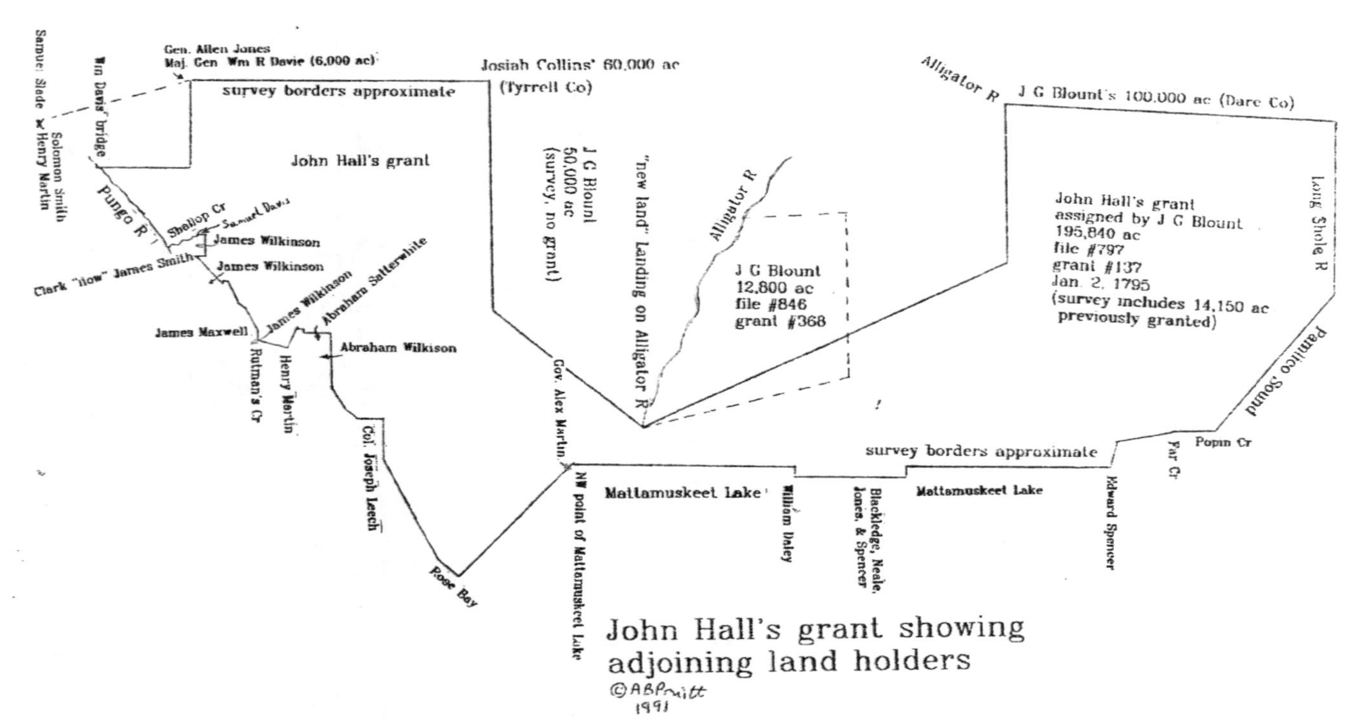

Samuel Slade
Solomon Smith
Henry Martin
Win Davis' bridge
Gen. Allen Jones
Maj. Gen Wm R Davie (6,000 ac)
survey borders approximate
Josiah Collins' 60,000 ac
(Tyrrell Co)
Alligator R
J G Blount's 100,000 ac (Dare Co)
John Hall's grant
Pungo R
Shellop Cr
Samuel Davis
James Wilkinson
James Wilkinson
Clark "now" James Smith
James Wilkinson
Abraham Satterwhite
James Maxwell
Rutman's Cr
Henry Martin
Abraham Wilkison
Col. Joseph Leech
Rose Bay
J G Blount
50,000 ac
(survey, no grant)
"new land" Landing on Alligator R
Alligator R
J G Blount
12,800 ac
file #846
grant #368
John Hall's grant
assigned by J G Blount
195,840 ac
file #797
grant #137
Jan. 2, 1795
(survey includes 14,150 ac
previously granted)
Long Shole R
Pamlico Sound
Gov. Alex Martin
NW point of Mattamuskeet Lake
Mattamuskeet Lake
William Daley
Blackledge, Neale,
Jones, & Spencer
Mattamuskeet Lake
survey borders approximate
Far Cr
Popm Cr
Edward Spencer
John Hall's grant showing
adjoining land holders
© A B Pruitt
1991

# Hyde County, NC Land Entries 1778-1795

[on the cover] Hyde Co Entry Book "Book B 1778"   [1778-1780]
page 1   An Account of the several land entries received by Edward Hancock, Hyde Co Entry taker, Feb. 23, 1778

1. Feb. 23, 1778 Thomas Gaylard enters 100 ac; border: Joseph Gurganus' corner, runs N16E to Layd's line, with Layd's line to Jonathan Gurganus' line, with Jonathan Gurganus' line to Thomas Gailard's line, & with his line to the beginning; "this entry at first run" N20W to Layd's line but by order of Court altered and "it as it now stands"; Jun. 9, 1778 caveated by William Hollowell; "tuck" back "his" money Aug. 31, 1778 and "tuck" up his bond.

2. Feb. 23, 1778 Jonathan Gurganus [or Garganus] enters 100 ac in Hyde Co on N side of Broad Cr; border: Thomas Gayland's line on Broad Cr, runs N with his line to Jonathan Gurganus' line, with that line to Broad Cr, & down the creek to the beginning.

page 2
3. Feb. 23, 1778 Benjamin Gaylard enters 50 ac in Hyde Co on W side of Pungo R and on E side of Pontegon Cr; border: Stephen Gaylard's corner, runs W along Back Swamp to benjamin Flinn's line, S of said line to Enward Swamp, E with the swamp to Stephen Gaylard's line, & with his line to the beginning.

4. Feb. 23, 1778 John Egleton enters 150 ac; border: near Beaufort Co line, on N side of Pungo Swamp, & Back Dismal "as has been surveyed and in possession" of John Egleton; known as Prices Ridge; this entry proved to be in "Buford" Co and said John Egleton "tuck" back his money for the same.

5. Feb. 23, 1778 Stephen Galard enters 25 ac in Hyde Co on E side of Pontegoe Cr and in Back Pocoson; border: runs N 40 poles from a pine to a pine, E 100 pols to a pine, S 40 poles to a pine, & W 100 poles to the beginning.

page 3
6. Feb. 23, 1778 Stephen Gaylard enters 425 ac in Hyde Co on N side of Machapungo R and E side of Pantego Cr; border: William Mixon's corner gum in "the" swamp, runs along Flinn's patent, N74E 194 poles to a pine on "the" side of Mill Br, with another of "his" patents, N74E 400 poles to Thomas Gayland's corner by "the" swamp side, runs S85E 400 poles with his line to Jones' corner, with his line S46W 90 poles, N80W 335 poles, S74W 160 poles, S45W 410 poles to Mixon's corner, & with Mixon's line N80W 220 poles to the beginning.

7. Feb. 23, 1778 Benjamin Hollowell enters 450 ac in Hyde Co on W side of Broad Cr; between Moses Winby sr, William Price's former line, & Henry Eborn's former line; the "greatest" part in "the" pecoson.

8. Feb. 23, 1778 John Gaylard enters 150 ac in Hyde Co on N side of Broad Cr and W side of Pung [sic] R; border: John Gaylard's line at "the" old road, runs NE, NW, W to John Gaylard's line, & with his line to the beginning.

page 4
9. Feb. 25, 1778 Thomas Jones enters 600 ac in Hyde Co on S side of Pungo R; border: near the head of the river, near Benjn Russell's line, runs SW to the back pocoson, NW up said pocoson, NE to the river, & With the river to the beginning; includes Grapevine Ridge and Moses Ridge.

10. Feb. 26, 1778 James Eborn enters 100 ac in Hyde Co; border: said Eborn's line on Pungo Cr, runs N40° 320 poles "across from that corner" to Moses Winley, & down Winley's line to the beginning.

11. Feb. 27, 1778 Caleb Chambers enters 100 ac in Hyde Co; border: a "lettel" glade on John Chambers' line, runs along said line to Joshua Foreman's line, to James Webster's line, along Webster's line to my own line, & along my own line to the beginning.

page 5
12. Mar. 2, 1778 Richard Capps enters 70 ac in Hyde Co on Hudley's Cr; border: runs along Thomas Jordan's line to Thomas Whright's line, to Thomas Bailey's line, along said Bailey's line to Jesse Bailey's line, to "his" corner, & down "the" marsh to the beginning.

13. Mar. 2, 1778 Benjamin Stedman enters 70 ac in Hyde Co at the head of Prices Cr; border: runs down said creek to the old "plantation" line known as Sinclear's "plantation", runs with that "patent" to "the" Savanah, across to "the" road, & along the road to the beginning.

14. Mar. 9, 1778 Thomas Smith enters 120 ac in Hyde Co; border: the mouth of Broad Cr on W side, runs up said creek to said Smith's "plantation", & with said Smith's line to the beginning.

page 6
15. Mar. 9, 1778 Hosey [or Hosea] Martin enters 640 ac in Hyde Co; border: on N side of "the" river swamp 100 poles W of the "plantation" where Solomon Smith lives, runs N5E 320 poles from a "sipras" in the swamp to a poplar on "the Grait Bend of Redes", W5N 320 poles to the beach, S5W 320 poles to the river swamp, & down the run of the river swamp to the beginning.

16. Mar. 28, 1778 Soloman Smith enters 300 ac in Hyde Co; border: runs E "some distance" from a "sipras on the" river swamp, then N 320 poles, W to the river swamp, & S to the beginning.

17. Apr. 4, 1778 Stephen Smith enters 75 ac in Hyde Co; border: Swaring Point, runs S to Joshua Smith's line, with his line to "the" river swamp, to the river, & along the river to the beginning.

page 7
18. May 29, 1778 William Sattarthwaite enters 100 ac in Hyde Co; border: Benjaman Russel's upper line on W side of Pungo R, runs N45W to "the bed of gallberes", W20S, N45E, & to the beginning.

19. Jun. 20, 1778 Jeremiah Gaylard enters 300 ac in Hyde Co; border: Thomas Topping's line on NE side of Broad Creek Swamp, runs W to the head of the swamp, down said swamp opposite "the" upper "plantation", S crossing the swamp, E to Jeremiah Gaylard's line, & with said line to the beginning.

20. Jun. 20, 1778 Jeremiah Gaylard enters 50 ac in Hyde Co; border: said Gaylard's line on S side of Ozbens Br, crosses said branch, & runs E to Gaylard's line.

page 8
21. Jun. 21, 1778 Jonathan Garganus enters 100 ac in Hyde Co on E side of Broad Cr; border: his "one" corner, runs NW with the old "mane rode" to Daniel Hallon's former line, SE with Hallon's line to my own line, & with my own line to the beginning; warrants "gone".

22. Aug. 17, 1778 George Davenport enters 400 ac in Hyde Co; border: Solomon Smith's corner at Lake Swamp, runs up said swamp 400 poles, NW to Hose Martin's line, down said line to Solomon Smith's line, & to the beginning; warrant out.

23. Sept. 1, 1778 William Watson enters 100 ac in Hyde Co on S side of Mathamuskat Lake; border: a cypress on the back line of Caleb Swindell, runs S 100 poles, & then runs parallel with Swindell's line; warrant out.

page 9
24. Sept. 1, 1778 Bartha Latham enters 600 ac in Hyde Co on the head of Pungo R; border: a cypres in the fork of the river that leads to Elbo Lake "East", runs up the fork swamp that leads to the lake N80E 320 poles to a beach, S 286 poles to a pine in the ready ground, W 320 poles to the run of "the" river swamp, & to the beginning; warrant out.

25. Sept. 10, 1778 John Poole enters 100 ac in Hyde Co; border: John Hamilton's corner, runs on the drean of "the" branch of Deep Cr in New Currituck, with Mark Rew's line South, with Silverthorm to Bell Fortsyne's line, to John Rew's, & with John Rew's line to the beginning; warrant out.

26. Sept. 10, 1778 John Potter enters 50 ac in Hyde Co; border: [in] New Currituck and between John Rew, Simon Fortsyne, James Hamilton, & Hezekiah Slade; warrant out.

page 10
27. Sept. 21, 1778 Bothas [or Rathas] Latham enters 100 ac in Hyde Co at the head of Pantego Cr; border: a corner of Benjn Flinn and Phinneis Latham, on E side of "the" pocoson, runs N 100 poles, W to Phaneius Latham's corner on the head of Deep Run, & along Phaineus Latham's line to the beginning; warrant out.

28. Sept. 29, 1778 George Duke enters 200 ac in Hyde Co; border: [mouth of--lined out] a branch between James Jones and George Duke, runs SE to William Davis's line, to "the" river swamp, & with the river swamp to the beginning; Dec. 8, 1778 Mr. Jacob Paul claims a "prioer wright" [prior right] to 100 ac of this entry; the jury allowed George Duke's entry good; Court ordered a warrant "out" May term 1779; warrant out.

29. Sept. 29, 1778 James Jones enters 200 ac in Hyde Co; border: the mouth of a branch between James Jones and George Duke, runs W about 2 miles, N to "the" river swamp, & down the river swamp to the beginning; warrant out.

page 11
30. Sept. 29, 1778 Peter McWilliams enters 200 ac in Hyde Co; border: in "the" swamp, a small gum near Solomon Smith "Purth", runs S "sum thing", W along Galberry's line about 0.5 "and" 0.25 mile, ESE to James Jones' line, down his line to "the" river swamp, & from Jones' line to the beginning; warrant out; "taken off".

31. Oct. 4, 1778 Jacob Paul enters 100 ac in Hyde Co; border: William Daves's corner on "the" river swamp, runs N60W 83 poles, S45W 200 poles to Davis's corner on Back Swamp, & along said Davis' line to the beginning; warrant out.

32. Oct. 6, 1778 William Satterthwaite enters 200 ac in Hyde Co on E side of Pungo R; border: Lake Swamp, runs N 0.5 miles, W to Solomon Smith's line, down Smith's line, & "cross" to the beginning.

page 12
33. Oct. 12, 1778 Thomas Bedford enters 100 ac in Hyde Co on W side of Pungo R; border: a swamp near a corn field of Peter McWilliams, runs S "a quarter", W 200 poles, & joins Peter McWilliams; being the land Peter McWilliams bought of Saml Slade and sold to Thomas Bedford; warrant out.

34. Oct. 24, 1778 William Boshop enters 100 ac in Hyde Co on W side of Pungo R; border: "the" river swamp below said Bishop's Landing, runs SW to Back

Swamp, along Back Swamp to a great branch, down the branch to the river swamp, & up the river swamp to the beginning; warrant out.

35. Oct. 29, 1778 William Hollowell enters 400 ac in Hyde Co; border: Benjn Hollowell, Henry Eborn, & in the fork of Deep Run making out of Broad Cr; Nov. 17, 1778 Henry Eborn claims a "pryer wright" to the land entered by Wm Hollowell "meeing" 200 ac joining my old lines.

page 13
36. Oct. 29, 178 William Hollowell enters 100 ac in Hyde Co in the fork of Deep Run and on Pantego Cr; border: Benjn Martin and Phanius Latham on NE side of said creek; warrant out.

37. Oct. 29, 1778 William Campbell and Joseph Hancock enter 200 ac in Hyde Co on W side of Broad Cr; border: William Price and Benjn Hollowell; warrant out; Jan. 4, 1779 caveated by Rothan Latham "how" claims a "proyer wright"; caveated dismissed by order from Rotheas Lathom [sic].

38. Oct. 29, 1778 Jontahan Phillips enters 100 ac in Hyde Co on N side of Pungo R; border: Jonathan Phillips' corner pine, runs N 26 poles to a gum on Back Dismal, 400 poles along said swamp, S 26 poles to Gaylord's line, to the "other" line, & to the beginning; warrant out.

page 14
39. Oct. 29, 1778 George Denison enters 640 ac in Hyde Co at the head of Pungo R; border: George Devenport's NW corner, runs N 320 poles, S 320 poles, & W along Devenport's line to the beginning; warrant out.

40. Oct. 29, 1778 Abram Jones enters 400 ac in Hyde Co; border: near the mouth of and on W side of Indian Run, runs up the run West, then N to "the" river swamp, & with the swamp to to the beginning; Dec. 28, 1778 this entry claimed by Jeremiah Johnston; Abraham Jones jr [sic] gives up his claim.

41. Oct. 29, 1778 Timothy Moorey enters 300 ac in Hyde Co on W side of Pungo R; border: Thomas Jones' line near Back Pecoson, runs W to or near Cypris Swamp, SE, NE to William Satterthwaite's line, with his line to Jones' line, & along Jones' line to the beginning; warrant out.

page 15
42. Oct. 29, 1778 Jonathan Gurganas enters 100 ac in Hyde Co on NE side of Pantego Swamp; border: Benjn Martin's line, runs NE, NW, SW to said Martin's line, & with his line to the beginning; warrant out.

43. Nov. 2, 1778 Benjamin Sanderson enters 20 ac in Hyde Co; between my line and "the" river shore; warrant out.

44. Nov. 2, 1778 Benjn. Sanderson enters 300 ac on Cedar Cr and on NE side of Pungo R; border: his own corner, runs to S side of "the same", NW down said creek to the mouth of Sheds Cr, SW to Sandy Point, with Pungo R to said Sanderson's line, & with his line to the beginning; Dec. 15, 1778 Francis Morris claims 130 ac of this entry, it being his property by deed from James [Thomas--lined out] Clark to him; dismissed by Capt. Sanderson.

page 16
45. Nov. 10, 1778 John Egleton enters 100 ac in Hyde Co; border: John Windley's back line and "the" pecoson; Dec. 28, 1778 Mrs. Mapel Wirly caveats this entry; this entry proves to be "Mrs. Mapel Windly has drawn" his claim and recd his money Jan. 18, 1779.

46. Nov. 14, 1778 Henry Eborn enters 640 ac in Hyde Co; border: his corner tree on N side of Pungo Cr, runs to William Eborn's line, runs NE a mile, a mile to his old line, & with his "other" line to the beginning; warrant out.

47. Nov. 18, 1778 David Green enters 450 ac in Hyde Co on S side of Mathameokeet Lake; border: NW corner of "the" savanah, runs S across the savanah, E to the E end, N across the savanah, & to the beginning; warrant out.

page 17
48. Nov. 31, 1778 [sic] John Rew enters 450 ac in Hyde Co [in] New Currituck; border: at the head of Fortscue Cr, runs down N side of said creek, NE 0.75 miles, & to the beginning; Jan. 9, 1779 Jeremiah Juley claims this entry and has given bond according to law.

49. Nov. 30, 1778 John Ensley enters 300 ac on N side of Old Mattamuskeet Cr; border: the head of Midle cr, runs NW to N coner of James Davison's line, S with his line to Gibbs' line, along Gibbs' line to "awright" line, & to the beginning; warrant out

50. Dec. 8, 1778 William Davis enters 200 ac in Hyde Co; border: a great branch below "the" landing, runs W and N 320 poles with "the" swamp to a great branch, N 90 poles to "the" river swamp, & with the swamp to the beginning; warrant out.

page 18
51. Dec. 8, 1778 William Davis enters 100 ac in Hyde Co; border: my own line, runs SW, & SE to "the" river swamp; warrant out.

52. Dec. 16, 1778 Mrs. Maple Windly enters 200 ac in Hyde Co on N side of Pungo Swamp [Creek--lined out]; border: Roger Jones' patent and Seth [Church--lined out] Windley; known as Hooppool Ridge; warrant issued.

53. Dec. 16, 1778 George Barrow enters 100 ac in Hyde Co on S side of Pungo Cr; border: Henry Eborn, Ragil Thoroughgood, & my own land I had of William Eborn called the Deep Cod; warrant out.

page 19
54. Dec. 16, 1778 Moses Windly enters 300 ac in Hyde Co on E side of Pungo Swamp; border: my own line, runs N70E 240 poles, & then to James Eborn's corner of his new survey; warrant issued.

55. Dec. 15, 1778 [sic] Francis Morris enters 130 ac in Hyde Co on E side of Pungo R; border: the mouth of Seder Cr, runs up the creek to a glade, up the glade to a line of marked trees, & with the river to the beginning; being the land said Morris bought of James Clark; warrant issued.

56. Dec. 26, 1778 George Carter enters 100 ac in Hyde Co on S side of Pungo R; border: Richard Harvey's corner known as Poyney Grove, runs S, W, N to the river, & down the river swamp to the beginning; warrant out.

page 20
57. Dec. 28, 1778 Jeremiah Johnston enters 200 ac in Hyde Co on W side of Pungo R and N side of Indian Run; border: the fork of Indian Run, runs up the run to Fork Run Swamp, with "the" back swamp to William Bishop's line, across the river swamp, & down the swamp to the beginning.

58. Dec. 30, 1778 Littleton Wilkins [or Lettelton Wedkins] enters 125 ac in Hyde Co on W side of Pungo R; border: my old patent, Webster's, & Springs.

59. Dec. 30, 1778 Samuel Mandowell enters 200 ac in Hyde Co; border: my own land, William Davis's patent, Savanah Br, & runs down to Broad Cr; warrant out.

page 21
60. Dec. 30, 1778 James McCabe enters 100 ac in Hyde Co on E side of Pungo R; known as White Ouck Landing; border: below "the plantation" on the river swamp, runs E, N, W, & S to the beginning; warrant out.

61. Dec. 30, 1778 James McCabe enters 100 ac in Hyde Co on Oack Ridge and E side of Pungo R; border: "the" upper field, runs W, S, E, & N to the beginning; warrant out.

62. Dec. 30, 1778 Jasper Keech enters 100 ac in Hyde Co in Poiney Savanah; being the land I bought of Benjamin Cording; warrant out.

page 22
63. Jan. 2, 1779 Caleb Foriman [or Foroman] enters 200 ac in Hyde Co on S side of Pungo Cr; border: "West South" of Holley Ridge, runs SE to William

Moor's line, down Moor's back line to Wm Harris's line, down Harris's back line to Benjn Martin's line, & along said line to the beginning; warrant out.

64. Jan. 2, 1779 John Eborn enters 100 ac in Hyde Co in Lorril Swamp and in Poiney Savanah; border: Henry Eborn and James Keech; warrant out.

65. Jan. 2, 1779 Jasper Keech enters 50 ac in Hyde Co; border: his own line, runs to Turky Br, & with "other courses"; warrant out.

pages 23
66. Jan. 2, 1779 James McCabe 100 ac in Hyde Co on E side of Pungo R; border: below "the plantation", runs E, N, W to the river swamp, & S to the beginning; known as Grassey Ridge; warrant out.

67. Jan. 2, 1779 Jacob Paul enters 100 ac in Hyde Co on W side of Pungo R; below "the plantation", runs SW to the "roode", & with the "rood" to Indian Run Swamp.

68. Jan. 6, 1779 Winfeild Gaylard enters 300 ac in Hyde Co on E side of Pantego Cr [Pungo R--lined out]; border: Thomas Gaylord's corner tree, runs S89E 185 poles to his line, S 18 poles to Jones' corner, S44W 160 poles, then to Stephen Gaylord's corner of his new survey, & N 43 poles to the beginning; warrant out.

page 24
69. Jan. 7, 1779 Mr. John Eborn enters 200 ac in Hyde Co; border: Thomas Barrow's old line and runs as far as the vacant land to contain 200 ac; warrant out.

70. Jan. 7, 1779 Mark Rew enters 100 ac in Hyde Co [in] New Currituck; border: W corner of Able Tuley; held formerly by Bailey McCartey "left to" Leah Anderson; warrant out.

71. Jan. 7, 1779 Thomas Adams enters 285 ac in Hyde Co on Shallow Cr; border: Arnols Ridge "East and South"; known as Arnal's land; warrant out.

page 25
72. Jan. 7, 1779 Mathaw Capps enters 100 ac in Hyde Co at Oack Ridge, at he head of Poiney Ridge, & on E side of Pungo R; warrant out.

73. Jan. 9, 1779 James Gaylord enters 150 ac in Hyde Co on S side of Pungo R and near George Duke Ridge; border: runs E 250 poles from a pine to John Winfild's line, S 125 poles to a pine, W 225 poles to a pine, & 40 poles to the beginning; warrant issued.

74. Jan. 9, 1779 William McCabe enters 150 ac "or more if vacant" in Hyde Co on W side of Pungo R; between William Davis and Great Br; warrant issued.

page 26
75. Jan. 11, 1779 John Loyd enters 200 ac in Hyde Co on Pantego Swamp; border: a little branch on S side of said creek, runs SW 0.25 miles, West North" to Capt. Bothas latham's line, & with said line to the run of the swamp.

76. Jan. 13, 1779 Thomas Easter enters 200 ac in Hyde Co on E side of Pungo R; border: the mouth of a gut [branch--lined out] opposite Juells Point "of marsh", runs up a glade, & runs along a line of ash [or "ass"] trees marked; contains the land I bought of Benja Slade as a deed will show and the vacant land between me and Enoch Slade "division line"; warrant out.

77. Jan. 15, 1779 John Fortsine enters 100 ac in Hyde Co on E side of Pungo Cr and Sheds Cr; between Charles Smith Cr and Seder Cr; warrant out.

page 27
78. Jan. 17, 1779 John Mark Harvey enters 640 ac in Hyde Co on Mathewskeet [Lake] and W side of Waseoking Cr; known as Mulbrey Ridge; warrant out.

79. Jan. 18, 1779 John Egelton enters 100 ac in Hyde Co; border: Moses Windley's new entry, his father's old line, Seth Windley, & Mapel Windley's new entry; warrant out.

80. Feb. 9, 1779 Valinetine Jasper enters 128 ac in Hyde Co in New Currituck; between Thomas Easter and Chapple formerly King Georges Cr; warrant out.

page 28
81. Feb. 22, 1779 William Russell enters 50 ac in Hyde Co in New Currituck; border: Robert Palmer's line on the head of Smiths Cr, Russell's line, & Jones; warrant out.

82. Feb. 22, 1779 James Hamilton enters 100 ac in Hyde Co in New Currituck; border: his own line on Sluds Cr, runs on Sluds Cr, on E side of Edmons Cr, Wm Fortscue's line, & Mathiaus Tyson's line.

83. Feb. 22, 1779 William Satterthwait enters 250 ac in Hyde Co; border: Thomas Jones' upper corner tree, runs NW 0.5 miles, NE, down to "the" river swamp, runs with the swamp to the "other" corner tree, & with Jones' line to the beginning; warrant out.

page 29
84. Feb. 22, 1779 Jeremiah Tuley enters 550 ac in Hyde Co in New Currituck; border: the head of Indian Cr and runs along the old line of marked trees; includes the land Mr. Simon Fortiscue patented; warrant out.

85. Jun. 1, 1779 Joseph Hancock and William Campbel enter 120 ac; border: their former entry in Hyde Co, back of Price's survey, on W side of Pungo R, & W side of Broad Cr; warrant out.

86. Jun. 1, 1779 James Eborn enters 150 ac in Hyde Co on W side of Pungo R and N side of Pungo Cr; border: Purkins' line on the creek swamp, runs to "the" back line, to the back line of Joel Martin's patent, down the line to the creek swamp, and to the beginning; warrant out.

page 30
87. Jun. 1, 1779 John Fortescue jr enters 200 ac in Hyde Co on N side of Pungo R and S side of Slades Cr; border: the mouth of Ducking Cr, runs down Slades Cr to Ash Cr, up Ash Cr, joins James Hambleton's line "to" Ann Banks' line, along Banks' line to another line to James Hambleton, down Hambleton's line to Ducking Cr, & to the beginning; warrant out.

88. Jun. 8, 1779 Benjamin Hollowell enters 200 ac in Hyde Co on W side of Pungo R, W side of Broad Cr, & E side of Windley's Savannah; known as Langly's "Ride"; caveated by Joseph Handcock and William Campbell.

89. Jun. 14, 1779 James Hambleton enters 40 ac in Hyde Co on E side of Pungo R and S side of Slade Cr; border: on Ducking Cr at a sedar post at the mouth of a small gut, runs to an "iron oak" post at the end of a ditch, to a sassafras post in "the" branch, up the branch to a line of marked trees, along the trees to Benjamin Slade's line, along Slade's line to Ducking Cr, & down the creek to the beginning; warrant out.

page 31
90. Jun. 14, 1779 Reuben Bartee enters 640 ac on E side of Pungo R; border: NE of Soloman Smith and S & W end of Northeast Ridge; warrant out.

91. Jun. 14, 1779 Samuel Slade enters 640 ac in Hyde Co on E side of Pungo R; border: Reuben Bartee's survey; warrant out.

92. Jul. 13, 1779 Littleton Wilkins enters 150 ac in Hyde Co on W side of Pungo R; within my old lines; border: a white gum in "the" purcosen and runs down said river; caveated by Seth Hover; this entry is set aside by "Littlton" Wilkins.

page 32
93. Jul. 19, 1779 William Watson enters 50 ac in Hyde Co on S side of Mattamuskeet Lake; border: White and Sivindell; warrant out.

94. Jul. 19, 1779 Israel Watson enters 200 ac in Hyde Co on S side of Mattamuskeet Lake; border: William Watson, Swindal, & William Watson's

former line; caveated by Caleb Swindell; the jurors upon trial find for Caleb Swindel a general verdict.

95. Jul. 23, 1779 William Thorrington enters 100 ac in Hyde Co on N side of Mattamuskeet Lake; border: William Porter's W corner, Stephen Brooke, & James Clayton; warrant out.

page 33
96. Aug. 12, 1779 James Watson enters 70 ac in Hyde Co on S side of Mattamuskeet Lake; border: Israel Watson and runs along Caleb Swindel's back line to William Watson's line; caveated by Caleb Swindel; the jury upon "tryal" find for Caleb Swindel a general verdict.

97. Aug. 17, 1779 William Turner enters 150 ac in Hyde Co on the head of Juniper Bay; warrant out.

98. Aug. 18, 1779 Abraham Jones enters 640 ac in Hyde Co on W side of Wesockin Cr, on Lightwood Cr, & runs W; warrant out.

page 34
99. Aug. 30, 1779 William Russell enters 400 ac in Hyde Co on Deep Bay and on Narrow Marshes [sic]; border: Benjamin Mason; warrant out "Aug. 8".

100. Aug. 30, 1779 William Carrowon [or Carronon] enters 200 ac in Hyde Co on S side of Mattamuskeet Lake; border: Joseph Weston's line "standing in" Robert Hodges' line; warrant issued.

101. Sept. 29, 1779 Isaac Swindell enters 200 ac in Hyde Co on N side of Mattamuskeet Lake; between John Swindell and William Palmer; warrant out.

page 35
102. Oct. 4, 1779 Solomon Jones and Nathan Sibly enter 100 ac in Hyde Co above the head of Juniper Cr and near Pungo Bluff; warrant out.

103. Oct. 9, 1779 James Jones enters 200 ac in Hyde Co on W side of Pungo R; border: my former entry; warrant out.

104. Oct. 9, 1779 James Jones enters 200 ac in Hyde Co on W [North--lined out] side of "Pung" R, W side of Indian Run, above Ford Run, & in the fork of Indian Run and Ford Run; Dec. 19, 1779 caveated by Abram Banks; Feb. 28, 1789 James Jones withdrew his entry and has taken his money back.

page 36
105. Oct. 12, 1779 David Davis enters 200 ac in Hyde Co on N side of Juniper Bay and on Oak Ridges; warrant out.

106. Oct. 18, 1779 John Mordick enters 50 a in Hyde Co on W side of Pungo R; between Benjamin Mordick, Daniel Martin, & Lazarus Foreman; warrant out.

107. Oct. 18, 1779 John Mordick enters 25 ac in Hyde Co on W side of Pungo R; border: Daniel Martin, Benjamin Mordick, & Richard Capps; warrant out.

page 37
108. Oct. 29, 1779 William Turner enters 640 ac in Hyde Co on the head of Juniper Bay; border: back of my former entry; warrant out.

109. Nov. 5, 1779 Abraham Gallaway enters 200 ac in Hyde Co on N side of Pantego Swamp; border: on S side of Benjamin Martin's line, Rotheas Latham, & the back puroson; warrant out.

110. Nov. 5, 1779 Frances Gallaway enters 200 ac in Hyde Co in Hyde Co on N side of Pantego Cr; border: Winfield Gaylard's corner, runs along John Windfield's corner, runs along John Windfield's line to Piney Swamp, along the swamp to Winfield Gaylard's line, & with his line to the beginning; warrant out.

page 38
111. Nov. 5, 1779 Abraham Gallaway 200 ac in Hyde Co on S side of Pungo R; border: Richard Harvey's corner, runs with his line to Robert Windfield's line, & runs with Jones' line; warrant out.

112. Nov. 5, 1779 John Egleton enters 500 ac in Hyde Co on S side of Pantego Cr; border: John Loyd's new entry; warrant out.

113. Nov. 7, 1779 Stephen Smith enters 100 ac in Hyde Co on E side of Pungo R; border: his own corner on "the" side of "the" marsh, runs down the river marsh to Thomas Nash's line, & along his line to the purcosen; warrant out.

page 39
114. Nov. 7, 1779 William Hollowell enters 150 ac in Hyde Co on W side of Pungo R; border: his own line, Jonathan Philips, Darby McCarty, Joseph Leech's Beach Ridge patent, Joseph Hollowell, John Windfield, & to the beginning; warrant out.

115. Nov. 7, 1779 Moses Windley enters 80 ac in Hyde Co; being the surplus land in Purkins' patent "formerly" now Windley's patent; warrant out.

116. Nov. 9, 1779 William Eborne enters 125 ac in Hyde Co on N side of Pungo Cr; border: his front line; caveated by Henry Eborn; jury finds for Henry Eborn a general verdict.

pag 40

117. Nov. 25, 1779 Southy Rew enters 100 ac in Hyde Co on E side of Pungo R; between William Bell's line and Long Cr; warrant out; caveated by Dickson Bell; Feb. 21, 1780 [caveat] dismissed by said Dickson Bell.

118. Nov. 27, 1779 Zedikiah Swindell enters 100 a in Hyde Co on Mattamuskeet Lake; border: Josiah Swindell and runs on his line down the lake; warrant out.

119. Nov. 27, 1779 Enoch Slade enters 50 ac in Hyde Co on E side of Pungo R; between Valentine Jasper and Thos Easter; warrant out.

page 41
120. Nov. 27, 1779 Anthony Tuley enters 200 ac in Hyde Co on Cypres Swamp and on E prong of Counning Harbour Cr; warrant out.

121. Nov. 30, 1779 Richard Harvey enters 100 ac in Hyde Co on S side of Pungo R; border: Piney Swamp, runs to Jones' line, along Jonathan Satterthwait's line, & to the beginning; warrant out.

122. Dec. 10, 1779 John Bright enters 100 ac in Hyde Co on W side of Pungo R; border: W of Jacob Paul's entry and S end of Rays Ridge; warrant out.

page 42
123. Dec. 10, 1779 John Bright enters 50 ac in Hyde Co on E side of Pungo R; between Hosea Martin, Solomon Smith, & the river; warrant out.

124. Dec. 10, 1779 William Russel enters 50 ac in Hyde Co on E side of Pungo R and in Currituck Swamp; between Christopher Jones' line, William Russel's former entry, & Turley's line; warrant out "Aug. 8".

125. Dec. 16, 1779 Abraham Banks enters 100 ac in Hyde Co on W side of Pungo R and S side of Indian Run; border: Indian Run Bridge, runs out to the bay "ponthen", up the run to the oak "noul" below Hickary "Loul", to the mouth of Ford Run, & down Indian Run to the beginning; warrant out.

page 43
126. Dec. 20, 1779 Abraham Banks enters 200 ac in Hyde Co on W side of Pungo R, W side of Indian Run, above Ford Run, & in the fork of Indian Run and Ford Run; border: runs up Indian Run to upper end of White oak "Noals", to Ford Run Swamp, down the swamp to Ford Run, & to the beginning; warrant out.

127. Dec. 22, 1779 Benjamin Russel enters 200 ac in Hyde Co on E side of Pungo R; border: Robert Palmer and William Russell; warrant out.

128. Dec. 24, 1779 Littleton Wilkins enters 200 ac in Hyde Co on W side of Pungo R; within my old lines; warrant out.

page 44
129. Feb. 1, 1780 Aaron Cox enters 400 ac in Hyde Co on W side of Pungo R and in the fork of N Dividing Creeks; border: a pine at the head of a marsh "a gut", runs 160 poles up Lazarus Foreman's line, & SE to the head of Holidays Cr; warrant out.

130. Feb. 2, 1780 Jesse Allen enters 40 ac in Hyde Co on E side of Pungo R; between Richard Jarot's patent, Mathias Tison, & John Allen; caveated by Saml Davis.

131. Feb. 2, 1780 Jesse Allen enters 10 ac in Hyde Co on E side of Pungo R; between Henry Hussey and John Allen; caveated by Mary Hussey; jury finds for Mary Hussey a general verdict.

page 45
132. Feb. 3, 1780 Richard Capps enters 250 ac in Hyde Co on W side of Pungo R and on S side of Jordans Cr; border: Martin's patent, Hall's land, Jordan's patent, Jordans Cr, & another patent of "said" Lovick Martin; warrant out.

133. Feb. 7, 1780 William Hollowell enters 400 ac in Hyde Co on W side of Pungo R; border: his former entry John Windfield, Joseph Acollowell jr, & Joseph Leech; warrant out.

134. Feb. 7, 1780 Samuel Gurganus enters 50 ac in Hyde Co on W side of Pungo R; border: his own line, Thomas Gaylard, & Hack Purcosen; warrant out.

page 46
135. Feb. 10, 1780 William Windfield enters 200 ac in Hyde Co on W side of Pungo R; within the bounds of Jones' patent on W side of Dowry Cr; warrant out.

136. Feb. 21, 1780 Benjamin Russel enters 150 ac in Hyde Co on E side of Pungo R; border: John Smith's line near Silvesters Cr and Palmer's line; warrant out.

137. Feb. 28, 1780 Abraham Banks enters 50 ac in Hyde Co on W side of Pungo R and on S side of Indian Run; border: Chinkcopine Ridges; warrant out.

page 47
138. Feb. 28, 1780 Jesse Noah Baily enters 150 ac in Hyde Co on W side of the head of N Dividing Cr; border: James Baily's corner tree, runs to Philip Jolly's line, to William Moor's line; warrant out.

139. Feb. 28, 1780 Boaz Hammond enters 540 ac in Hyde Co on W side of N Dividing Creeks; border: Alexander Foreman and James Hamilton.

140. Feb. 28, 1780 John Fodree enters 300 ac in Hyde Co on the head of Swan Quarter Bay; border: Meeatry's Swamp line "from the marsh to the E corner".

page 48
141. Feb. 28, 1780 John Pool enters 250 ac in Hyde Co on Swan Quarter [Bay] and Lake Savannah.

142. Feb. 28, 1780 Elisha Morris enters 80 ac in Hyde Co on E side of Pungo R; border: Solomon Smith's S corner, runs S 80 poles, E 160 poles, & N 80 poles to Solomon Smith's line; warrant out.

143. Feb. 29, 1780 William Troop enters 100 ac in Hyde Co on W side of Pungo R; border: William Win's corner, runs with Cording's line to Sage's line, runs with Sage's line to Hollowel's [line], & down Hollowel's line to the beginning.

page 49
144. Feb. 29, 1780 John Abrams enters 100 ac in Hyde Co on W side of Pungo R and N side of N Dividing Creeks; border: Cox's corner, Mordick's line, runs along Mordick's line to Chambers's line, to the creek, & with the creek to the beginning.

145. May 30, 1780 William Eborn jr enters 300 ac in Hyde Co on E side of Pantego Cr; within and joins my old patent; warrant out.

146. May 30, 1780 William Eborn sr enters 125 ac in Hyde Co on N side of Pungo Cr; border: at the creek, runs up my new entry to my old line, up my old line, then E, NW, SW to James Eborn's line, down said line to the creek, down the creek to the beginning; caveated by Henry Eborn.

page 50
147. May 30, 1780 Caleb White enters 180 ac in Hyde Co on Mattamuskeet Lake; being the surplus land in my old line; warrant out.

148. Jul. 8, 1780 Samuel Chapman enters 640 ac in Hyde Co on the head of Pungo R; border: George Denison's new survey; warrant out.

149. Jul. 11, 1780 Benjamin Russel enters 320 ac in Hyde Co on E side of Pongo R; border: John Smith and his own land; warrant out.

page 51
150. Jul. 11, 1780 Reuben Bartee enters 640 ac in Hyde Co in Mattamuscat [Swamp]; border: on N side of Wappoping Point, at the head of Berrey's Cr, & at Jennet's corner; warrant out.

151. Jul. 11, 1780 Reuben Bartee enters 300 ac in Hyde Co in Mattamusceat [Swamp]; border: on E side of Wappoping [Point] and joins John Ensley.

152. Jul. 11, 1780 Joseph Hancock enters 640 ac in Hyde Co on the head of Swan Quarter [Bay]; border: William Thorroton's line on W; warrant out.

page 52
153. Jul. 13, 1780 Caleb Swindel enters 400 ac in Hyde Co on S side of Mattameskeet [Lake]; border: a sweet gum on the lake side, runs SE 80 poles, SW, NW to the lake, & with the lake to the beginning; warrant out.

154. Aug. 28, 1780 Reuben Slade enters 100 ac in Hyde Co on E side of Pungo R and W side of Silvesters Cr; border: Silvester's line on the creek, runs S72E with his line to the river, with the river to Silvesters Cr, & up the creek to the beginning; warrant out.

155. Aug. 28, 1780 William Carrowon enters 300 ac in Hyde Co on E side of Swan Quarter [Bay]; border: John Smith's W corner; includes David Davis's folly; warrant out.

page 53
156. Aug. 28, 1780 Charles Hetherington enters 100 ac in Hyde Co on S side of N Dividing Cr; between Eleaser Jackson and Levi Mordick; warrant out.

157. Aug. 29, 1780 William Russel enters 400 ac in Hyde Co on Pungo Bluf Marshes and on "Bluf Marshes"; border: "the" small bluf bay, runs W, & N; warrant out.

158. Aug. 29, 1780 William Russel enters 100 ac in Hyde Co on E side of Pungo R; border: his own line and the patent land of North & Coston; warrant out.

page 54
159. Aug. 29, 1780 Thomas Topping enters 200 ac in Hyde Co on N side of Broad Cr; border: Daniel Hollon, runs NW, & joins John Gaylord; warrant out "Nov. 30".

[on inside back cover of the book] $7 not paid by Abram, 11 shillings over paid by Gallaway [signed] Richard Capps

[The following entries are in the same folder but a second "book".]
Hyde Co Entry Book   from Nov. 1783 to Jul 1785
page 1
160 (1). Nov. 25, 1783 Augustin Spain enters 50 ac in Hyde Co on Northwest Cr which makes out of Juniper Bay and runs "towards the" old lake.

161 (2). Nov. 25, 1783 Abram Jones and John Eborn enter 600 ac in Hyde Co between the head of Juniper Bay and "the" lake; between David Green's lines and on both sides of the road from "the" bay to Juniper Bay.

162 (3). Nov. 25, 1783 John Jordan and John Eborn enter 300 ac on N side of Rows Bay; border: near the lines "obtained by" Mason.

163 (4). Nov. 25, 1783 Thomas Jordan enters 105 ac; border: Tolyes line in Hyde Co in New Currituck.

page 2
164 (5). Nov. 25, 1783 John Jordan enters 100 ac in New Currituck in Hyde Co; border: Toley's line; warrant out.

165 (6). Nov. 25, 1783 Thomas Jordan enters 120 ac in Hyde Co in New Currituck; border: Christopher Jones and Mason; warrant out.

166 (7). Nov. 25, 1783 Benjamin Hollowell enters 150 ac on Pantego Swamp on NW side, nearly a mile from the swamp, & near a Gum Swamp; being a ridge John Loyd "found"; warrant.

167 (8). Nov. 25, 1783 Benjamin Gaylard enters 500 ac between Pantego Swamp and the head of Pongo R; warrant.

page 3
168 (9). Dec. 6, 1783 Thomas Jordan enters 400 ac in Hyde Co in Leaurel Swamp; border: David Bailey and Jesse Bailey; Feb. 23, 1784 caveated by John Abrams; dismissed by the court.

169 (10). Dec. 3, 1783 Thomas Jordan enters 200 ac in Hyde Co in Leaurel Swamp; border: his former entry; warrant out.

170 (11). Dec. 3, 1783 Seth Hovey enters 250 ac on both sides of the road from Bath to Woodstock [Cr]; border: Nicholes Daws, John Webster, & John Harvey's patent; warrant.

171 (12). Dec. 9, 1783 John Hancock and Benjn Hollowell enter 140 ac; between William Price's former line, Danil. Hollon's former line, & Eleons Gurganis; warrant.

page 4
172 (13). Dec. 9, 1783 Richard Blackledge enters 640 ac in Hyde Co in the swamp between Currituck and Mattumusket [Lake]; warrant.

173 (14). Dec. 9, 1783 Thomas Jordan enters 10 ac in Hyde Co in Tarkiln Neck; warrant.

174 (15). Dec. 24, 1783 Solomon Smith enters 400 ac on W side of Pungo R and on Indian Run; border: runs "towards" Jas Winfield; warrant.

175 (16). Dec. 24, 1783 Solomon Smith enters 100 ac on W side of Pongo R; warrant.

page 5
176 (17). Dec. 24, 1783 Solomon Smith enters 200 ac on E side of Pong R; border: George Duke and runs "towards" Mathew Capps; warrant.

177 (18). Dec. 24, 1783 Solomon Smith enters 200 ac on W side of Pongo Lake; border: runs W from the old landing; warrant.

178 (19). Dec. 24, 1783 Solomon Smith enters 50 ac on W side of Pongo R; border: Richard Harvey and runs W; warrant.

179 (20). Dec. 24, 1783 Solomon Smith enters 100 ac; border: Abam Banks on W side of Pongo R; warrant.

page 6
180 (21). Dec. 25, 1783 Thomas Jordan enters 200 ac in Hyde Co on W side of Woodstock Cr; border: his old line; Mar. 20, 1784 caveated by James Cleeves; caveat drawn by "himself"; warrant.

181 (22). Dec. 25, 1783 Abram Wilkinson enters 200 ac on N side of Woodstock Cr and between Woodstock and Rutneys Creeks.

182 (23). Dec. 25, 1783 Abram Wilkinson enters 400 ac on S side of Woodstock Cr.

183 (24). Dec. 26, 1783 James Cleeves enters 640 ac on E side of Pongo R; border: John Tyson and James Wilkinson.

page 7
184 (25). Dec. 26, 1783 James Cleeves enters 200 ac in Hyde Co on S side of Woodstock Cr; border: Abram Wilkinson's back line; warrant.

185 (26). Dec. 26, 1783 James Cleeves enters 640 ac on E side of Pongo R; border: his former entry, James Wilkinson, & Abram Wilkinson; warrant.

186 (27). Dec. 26, 1783 James English enters 100 ac on the head of Juniper Bay; border: Wm Turner and David Green; warrant.

# Hyde County, NC Land Entries 1778-1795

187 (28). Dec. 26, 1783 William Thorington enters 100 ac on N side of Wapoping Cr; border: Saml Henry, Robert Jenet, & Thos Gibbs.

page 8
188 (29). Dec. 26, 1783 Peter Carter enters 500 ac; between Machpongo Bluf and Ezekiel Glen; warrant.

189 (30). Dec. 28, 1783 Jacob Paul enters 100 ac; border: William Davis, runs N up "the" river, Isaac Rogers, & Back Swamp; warrant.

190 (31). Dec. 29, 1783 Jacob Paul enters 50 ac; border: William Davis and runs NW up "the" river.

191 (32). Dec. 29, 1783 Jeremiah Johnson enters 100 ac; between his old lines and "the" river.

page 9
192 (33). Dec. 29, 1783 Solomon Smith enters 138 ac on NE side of Pongo R; border: runs E from the river and S to James McCabe's line at "the" white oaks.

193 (34). Jan. 1, 1784 Joel Davenport enters 50 ac; border: George Davenport and in the fork of "the" swamp.

194 (35). Jan. 1, 1783 Joel Davenport enters 50 ac in Indian Run Swamp; between Jeremiah Johnson and Solomon Smith.

195 (36). Dec. 2, 1784 [sic] Hosea Martin enters 150 ac on Pantego Cr and on "the" side of Pongo R; border: Chir. Letham, Rotheas Lotham, & Benj Flin; warrant out.

page 10
196 (37). Jan. 2, 1784 Richard Blackledge enters 640 ac in Hyde Co in the swamp between Rows Bay and Mattimuskeet Lake; warrant.

197 (38). Jan. 2, 1784 John Webster enters 80 ac; border: Winn, Nicholas Daws, & Wm Webster; warrant.

198 (39). Jan. 3, 1784 Rotheas Latham enters 200 ac on Pantego Cr and on the head of Deep Run; border: his own line, Benjn Martin, & Phineas Latham.

199 (40). Jan. 3, 1784 Hosea Martin enters 170 ac in Hyde Co on Pongo R and on the head of Arthurs Cr.

page 11
200 (41). Jan. 4, 1784 Richard Harvey enters 25 ac on the Great Swamp Cosway; border: at Burges's line, runs to Abram Gallow's line, along said line to

Robert Winfield's line, to Col. Leach's line, & with Leach's line to the beginning; warrant.

201 (42). Jan. 6, 1784 James Winfield enters 100 ac on W side of Machpongo R; border: on the river above the "plantation" where he lives; warrant.

202 (43). Jan. 9, 1784 James Wilkinson enters 100 ac on the head of Depps Cr; border: Nash and Jas Wilkinson; warrant.

203 (44). Feb. 1, 1784 John Eborn and Edward McSwain enter 100 ac on Pantego Swamp; between John Loyd and Benjn Martin's patents; warrant.

page 12
204 (45). Feb. 1, 1784 Edward McSwain enters 80 ac on E side of Machpongo R; border: N corner of Solomon Smith's patent; warrant.

205 (46). Feb. 3, 1784 John Wilkinson enters 200 ac on W side of Pongo R; border: Back Swamp, Jacob Paul, & John Daves; being the land he lives on; warrant.

206 (47). Feb. 3, 1784 Benjn Rogers enters 100 ac; border: his lower corner, runs NE to "the" main river, up to Tho Jones' line, & joins the land where he lives.

207 (48). Feb. 3, 1784 Benj Rogers enters 320 ac; border: John Daves and Back Swamp.
page 13
208 (49). Feb. 3, 1784 Benj Rogers enters 250 ac on E side of Pongo R; border: Rotheas Latham; warrant.

209 (50). Feb. 7, 1784 Rotheas Latham enters 60 ac; border: Lemount's beginning corner, runs to Arthur Hollowell's corner, with Hollow's [sic] line to Wilkin's line, with Wilkin's line to his own line that he bought of John Webster, with Harvey's line to Lermount's line, & with Lermount's line to the beginning; warrant.

210 (51). Feb. [omitted], 1784 John Caps enters 10 ac; border: his own line in Piney Point; warrant.

211 (52). Feb. 7, 1784 Christopher Mason enters 50 ac; border: Morris Mason and in Currituck; Apr. 5 caveated by Sam Mason; caveat drawn by himself; warrant.

page 14

212 (53). Feb. 7, 1784 Malika Burges enters 30 ac; border: the front land I now possess, at my first corner near Jarves's Cr, runs S72E 213 poles, N50W 113 poles, & to the beginning; warrant.

213 (54). Feb. 9, 1784 Zachariah Barrow enters 200 ac; border: in the porcosion back of George Barrow's back line and George Barrow jr's line; warrant.

214 (55). Feb. 16, 1784 Benj Flin enters 50 ac on Pantego Cr; border: his old line on N side of his "plantation"; warrant.

215 (56). Feb. 16, 1784 Richard Blackledge enters 640 ac in the swamp between Currituck and Mattemeskeet [Lake].

page 15
216 (57). Feb. 17, 1784 Richard Blackledge enters 640 ac in Hyde Co and between Currituck and Mattemeskeet [Lake]; warrant.

217 (58). Feb. 17, 1784 Richard Blackledge enters 640 ac in Hyde Co in the swamp between Currituck and Mattemeskeet [Lake]; warrant.

218 (59). Feb. 17, 1784 Richard Blackledge enters 640 ac in Hyde Co in the swamp between Currituck and Mattemeskeet [Lake]; warrant.

219 (60). Feb. 17, 1784 Richard Blackledge enters 640 ac in Hyde Co in the swamp between Currituck and Mattemeskeet [Lake]; warrant.

page 16
220 (61). Feb. 17, 1784 Richard Blackledge enters 640 ac in Hyde Co in the swamp between Currituck and Mattemeskeet [Lake]; warrant.

221 (62). Feb. 17, 1784 Rich. Blackledge enters 640 ac in Hyde Co in the swamp between Currituck and Mattemeskeet [Lake].

222 (63). Feb. 17, 1784 Rich. Blackledge enters 640 ac in Hyde Co between Currituck and Matemuskeet [Lake].

223 (64). Feb. 17, 1784 Richard Blackledge enters 640 ac in Hyde Co between Currituck and Matemuskeet [Lake].

page 17
224 (65). Feb. 24, 1784 William Palmer, John Mason, & John Kirkonell enter 360 ac; border: W of "Mot" Timothy Cove's on the reaf at the East end of "the" lake, runs N with the lake opposite Cutrel's line, with "the different" lines to the Indian line, with said line to Timothy Cove, & to the beginning; warrant.

225 (66). Feb. 24, 1784 Zenos Eborn enters 150 ac on W side of Pongo Cr; border: W of George Barrow's new survey, on W side of "his" mill pond, & runs W to Back Porcosion; warrant.

226 (67). Feb. 24, 1784 Reuben Slade enters [omitted] ac in Hyde Co on E side of Pongo R; border: said Slade's line where it joins John Smith's patent, runs with Smith's line to Fork Cr, along Fork Cr to Wm Russell's line, with Russell's line to Silvester's line, with Silvester's line to Rolin Slade' line, & to the beginning; warrant.

227 (68). Mar. 5, 1784 Jeremiah Tooly enters 560 ac in Currituck on Swan Island Marshes; within the line of John Tooley's patent.

page 18
228 (69). Mar. 5, 1784 Jeremiah Tooley enters 250 ac in Currituck; border: John Mason's line, runs with a line of marked trees down to the head of Nockinghammak Cr, with the creek and bay to John Tooley's line, & with his line to the beginning; warrant.

229 (70). Mar. 12, 1784 Sothey Rew enters 250 ac on the head of Nocking Hammock Cr; border: Jeremiah Tooley's entry; includes a place known as the High Woods; warrant.

230 (71). Mar. 12, 1784 Jesse Allin enters 40 ac in Hyde Co; being part of the land in John Rigney's patent on S side of Oyster shel Cr; "which land is liable for want of an hur to be taken"; warrant.

231 (72). Mar. 12, 1784 Caleb Foreman enters 100 ac on N side of Pongo Cr; within "the call of" 500 ac granted to Joshua Foreman.

page 19
232 (73). Mar. 12, 1784 Daniel Danels enters 90 ac on S side of "the" new land; border: John Swindel; warrant.

233 (74). Mar. 12, 1784 Elisabeth Silvester enters 100 ac on E side of Pongo R; border: her beginning corner on Smiths Cr, runs with said line to the river, & with the river and creek to the beginning; Mar. 16, 1784 by Jas Cleves.

234 (75). Mar. 12, 1784 Enoch Flinn enters 25 ac on E side of Pantego Cr; border: Flinn; warrant.

235 (76). Mar. 12, 1784 Edward McSwain enters 45 ac on Severn Cr; border: Robert Molin's patent.

page 20

236 (77). Mar. 12, 1784 William Hollowell enters 25 ac on E side of Pantego Cr and in Jacks Neck; border: Jones, William Websten [sic], Geden, Isrel Wilkinson, & Jos Hollowell; warrant.

237 (78). Mar. 12, 1784 Seth Fortescue enters 50 ac on N side of N Dividing Cr and on the head of Holloways Gut; warrant.

238 (79). Mar. 12, 1784 Nathan Harvey enters 12 ac on E side of N Dividing Cr and on Pampli corner.

239 (80). Mar. 14, 1784 James Cleeves enters 86 ac; between the river and Silvester's patent in Currituck; border: Elisabeth Silvester's entry.

page 21
240 (81). Mar. 14, 1784 Augustin Spain enters 150 ac; border: his old entry number 1 [see No. 160 above]; warrant.

241 (82). Mar. 14, 1784 Josiah Jarves enters 500 ac on E side of Swan Quarter Bay; border: the head of Oyster Cr, runs round N side of "Poast" oak Ridge to the E end, S to Josiah Jarves' line, with his line to Oyster Cr, & up the creek to the beginning; warrant.

242 (83). Mar. 14, 1784 Josiah Jarves enters 410 ac; border: E end of Chinkopin Ridge, runs [on] N side of the ridge to his former entry, with said entry to Josiah Jarves' line, with his entry down to Juniper Bay, with the water to the head of Rattlesnake Cr, & to the beginning; warrant.

243 (84). Mar. 14, [omitted] Thomas Malison enters 25 ac on N side of N Dividing Cr; border: his old line.

page 22   [blank page]

page 23
244 (85). Mar. 15, 1784 William Albert enters 400 ac on N side of Juniper Cr; between David Green and Augustin Span; warrant.

245 (86). Mar. 15, 1784 William Davis enters 100 ac in Currituck on E side of Pongo R and on N side of "Oyter" shel Cr; border: John Davis' line, runs with Davis's line to Fortescue's line, with Fortescue's line to Banks' line, to Hamilton's line, with his line to Booty's line, to Alderson's line, Sanderson's line, to "Slake" Cr, down the creek to Davis' line, to the beginning; warrant.

246 (87). Mar. 15, 1784 Elizabeth Smith enters 50 ac on W side of Pongo R; border: Stephen Smith, Joshua Smith, McWilliams, & a branch; warrant.

247 (88). Mar. 15, 1784 James Hamilton 110 ac on E side of Pongo R and S side of Slades Cr; border: Richard Ballance's patent, James Hammilton's new grant, Booty, & Slades Cr.

page 24
248 (89). Mar. 16, 1784 Samuel Gurganis enters 50 ac on W side of Pongo R; border: Aron Gurganis's line and runs to Charles Leath's line on N side of "said" line; warrant.

249 (90). Mar. 16, 1784 Francis Cradell enters 500 ac on E side of "Swam" Quarter Bay; border: the head of Oyster Cr, runs down the creek N and W to Smith's line, & to the beginning.

250 (91). Mar. 16, 1784 James Cleeves enters 18 ac on E side of Pongo R; between Saml Leath and Richard Jordan.

251 (92). Mar. 16, 1784 Valentine Nehell enters 50 ac on Matimeskeet Lake; border: on "the" canell running by the [land--lined out] of Silvester "to be" the middle of "said" land, runs E and W along the boundary formed by the lake water where the Mattemusk Indians got a patent for ["blant"--lined out] acres, "to be" N boundary, & "to be" 200 yards N and S along the lake flats; warrant.

page 25
252 (93). Apr. 1, 1784 Enoch Flinn enters 30 ac; border: Benjn Gaylard, Stephen Gaylard, & Flinn; warrant.

253 (94). Apr. 1, 1784 Enoch Flinn enters 25 ac; border: Flinn on E side of Pantego Cr.

254 (95). Apr. 1, 1784 Richard Blackledge enters 640 ac between Currituck and Matemuskeet [Lake].
255 (96). Jul. 18, 1784 Joakim Eborn enters 100 ac on S side of Broad Cr; between Benjn Hollowell, Sam Mackduel, & Benjamin Barret.

page 26
256 (97). Sept. 14, 1784 Stephen Gaylard enters 400 ac between the head of Pongo R and Pantego Swamp.

257 (98). Sept. 14, 1784 Elisha Durden enters 50 ac on N side of Pongo R; between David Durden, Benjn Barnet, & Manduel.

258 (99). Sept. 14, 1784 Benj Gaylard [Fedrick Blunt--lined out] enters 40 ac on Pongo R; border: near Galloway's line.

259 (100). Oct. 6, 1784 Joseph Leach enters 600 ac between the head of Jones Cr and Dowrey Cr; border: SE end of his own land called Beach Ridge patent.

page 27
260 (101). Oct. 6, 1784 Joseph Leach enters 450 ac between the head of Jones Cr and Dowery Cr; border: SW of his own land called Beech Ridge patent.

261 (102). Oct. 6, 1784 Joshua Leach enters 160 ac on W side of Pongo R; being the front of his own land of 640 ac called the Bay patent.

262 (103). Oct. 6, 1784 John Jordan enters 12 ac; border: Levy Tooly and his own land.

263 (104). Oct. 6, 1784 Daniel Tyson enters 200 ac on W side of Pongo R; being part of the land formerly called Brite's land; border: Wm Win's patent and the "Bech" Ridge patent.

page 18
264 (105). Nov. 3, 1784 Saml Daves enters 50 ac where he lives; border: Tho Mack Williams [sic] near the Beach Ridge.

265 (106). Nov. 3, 1784 Thomas McWilliams enters 200 ac; where he lives; border: Samuel Davis.

266 (107). Nov. 30, 1784 Major Clark enters 25 ac on W side of Pongo R; border: on S side of Jones' patent.

267 (108). Nov. 30, 1784 Major Clark enters 100 ac on N side of Pongo R and W side of Jones Cr; border: Jones' patent.

page 29
268 (109). Nov. 30, 1784 William Hollowell enters 400 ac on Deep Run and Turkey Neck; border: back of Benjamin Hollowell's land, W of Broad Cr, Robert Barret, Henry Eborn, & Jas Eborn.

269 (110). Nov. 30, 1784 Richard Harvey [or Havey] enters 50 ac on W side of Pongo R; border: his own patent and runs to Green Swamp.

270 (111). Nov. 30, 1784 James Wilkinson enters 100 ac on E side of Pongo R; border: his own land and John Arthur.

271 (112). Nov. 30, 1784 James Wilkinson enters 300 ac on E side of Pongo R; border: Aron Cox, Abram Wilkinson, & Abram Satterwhite.
page 30
272 (113). Nov. 30, 1784 Jeremiah Gaylard enters 200 ac on Broad Creek Swamp; border: his own lines.

273 (114). Nov. 30, 1784 Jeremiah Gaylard enters 100 ac [on] Broad Creek Swamp; border: Elious Gurganes' former line.

274 (115). Nov. 30, 1784 Phineas Latham 300 ac on N side of Pantego Cr; border: Flin.

275 (116). Nov. 30, 1784 James Cleeves enters 40 ac on N side of Pongo R; within "the calls" [of] Saml Leath's patent on Slade Cr.

page 31
276 (117). Nov. 30, 1784 James Hamilton enters 50 ac on S side of Slade Cr; between the head of Ash Cr and Oyster shel Cr; border: William Davis and his own line.

277 (118). Dec. 12, 1784 Reuben Barter enters 218 ac; border: Malica Burges; within "the calls of" Silvester's patent.

278 (119). Dec. 12, 1784 John Winfield enters 120 ac on the head of Jones Cr; border: the beginning of Beech Ridge patent, runs to "the" Dowery patent, & to Brite's line.

279 (120). Dec. 21, 1784 David Durdin enters 50 ac on N side of Broad Cr; border: Manduel and Barnet.

page 32
279A (no number). [entered by mistake, no date or enterer's name] enters 200 ac on S side of Pantego Cr; border: Edward McSwain's patent.

280 (121). Dec. 27, 1784 John Loyd enters 40 ac; border: his own line and Pantego Swamp.

281 (122). Jan. 5, 1785 Vineard Campbell enters 200 ac on W side of Pantego Cr; border: [his own line--lined out] Edward MackSwain's [sic] patent.

282 (123). Jan. 6, 1785 Thomas Gaylard enters 45 ac; border: his old line, Moline's patent, & Jacob Wilkinson.

page 33
283 (124). Mar. 5, 1785 George Barrown enters 150 ac on W side of Pongo Cr; between his own lines; border: Zach Barrow's line of his new survey.

284 (125). Mar. 5, 1785 Elisha Durden enters 100 ac; border: William Winn and John Daves.

285 (126). May 30, 1785 Benjamin Gibbs sr and Richard Sanderson enter 300 ac in Matemiskeet [Swamp]; between the Indian line and the lake; border: near Molley Timothy Coves on N side of the Indian line.

286 (127). May 30, 1785 Richard Blackledge enters 100 ac on Broad Creek Swamp; warrant.

page 34
287 (128). May 30, 1785 Richard Blackledge enters 100 ac on Broad Creek Swamp; warrant.

288 (129). May 30, 1785 Richard Blackledge enters 100 ac on the swamp of Broad Creek Mills; warrant.

289 (130). May 30, 1785 Richard Blackledge enters 300 ac on Broad Creek Swamp; warrant.

290 (131). May 30, 1785 Richard Blackledge enters 300 ac on Mill Swamp and on Broad Cr; warrant.

page 35
291 (132). May 30, 1785 Richard Blackledge enters 300 ac on Broad Creek Swamp; warrant.

292 (133). May 30, 1785 Richard Blackledge enters 640 ac on Broad Creek Swamp; warrant.

293 (134). May 30, 1785 Richard Blackledge enters 640 ac on Broad Cr; warrant.

294 (135). May 30, 1785 Richard Blackledge enters 640 ac in Broad Creek Swamp.

page 36
295 (136). May 30, 1785 Richard Blackledge enters 640 ac in the swamp between Swan Quarter Bay and Matimeskeet Lake; warrant.

296 (137). May 30, 1785 Richard Blackledge enters 640 ac in the swamp between Swan Quarter Bay and Matimskeet Lake.

297 (138). May 30, 1785 Richard Blackledge enters 640 ac in Hyde Co in the swamp between Curituck and Matimuskeet [Lake].

298 (139). May 30, 1785 Richard Blackledge enters 640 ac in Hyde Co in the swamp between Juniper Bay and Matimuskeet [Lake].

page 37
299 (140). May 30, 1785 Richard Blackledge enters 640 ac in the swamp between Swan Quarter [Bay] and Matimeskeet [Lake].

300 (141). May 30, 1785 Richard Blackledge enters 640 ac; border: his former entry No. 138.

301 (142). May 30, 1785 Richard Blackledge enters 640 ac; border: his former entry No. 139.

302 (143). May 30, 1785 Richard Blackledge enters 640 ac in the swamp between Currituck and Mattimeskeet [Lake].

page 38
303 (144). May 30, 1785 Richard Blackledge enters 640 ac in the swamp between the lake and Juniper Bay.

304 (145). May 30, 1785 Richard Blackledge enters 640 ac in Dismal Swamp between Rows Bay and Mattimuskeet [Lake].

305 (146). May 30, 1785 Richard Blackledge enters 640 ac in "the" swamp between Rows Bay and Mattimuskeet [Lake].

page 39
306 (147). May 30, 1785 James Cleeves enters 86 ac on E side of Pongo R; border: Elisa [or Elisabeth] Silvester's entry; Jun. 1, 1785 caveated by Christopher Mason "purchase drawn".

307 (148). May 30, 1785 Edward McSwain enters 640 ac between the head of Pongo R and Pantego Cr.

308 (149). [no date] Zedekiah Swindel [or Swindal] enters 200 [written over 140] ac on Matimuskeet Lake.

309 (150). Jul. 21, 1785 Thomas Parker enters 640 ac on Swan Quarter [Bay]; border: Hancock, Fodrey, & Carrowone; [same entry written in and lined out at bottom of p. 38].

page 40   [blank page]

[on cover of third "book"]   "Hyde Entry Book"
[written at top of each sheet in this book:]   "Woodstock"
page 1
310 (1). Sept. 2, 1785 Joseph Leech enters 110 ac in Hyde Co; being an island in Matchpungo R, a "little" above "Logd" house Landing, & opposite Swearing Point; warrant out.

311 (2). Sept. 6, 1785 Joseph Leech enters 640 ac in Hyde Co between Pantigo Cr and Pongo R; border: Stephen Gaylard's new land; warrant out.

312 (3). Sept. 6, 1785 Joseph Leech enters 640 ac in Hyde Co between Broad Creek Swamp and Woodstock Creek Swamp; border: John Gray Blunt, James Cleves, & Abraham Wilkinson sr; warrant out.

313 (4). Sept. 6, 1785 Joseph Leech enters 400 ac in Hyde Co in New Currituck Swamp; border: Richard Palmer esq; warrant out.

314 (5). Sept. 7, 1785 Richard Harvey jr enters 40 ac in Hyde Co on W side of Mch. Pungo R; border: Robt Winfield, Major Clark, & Abraham Gallowey; warrant out.

page 2
315 (6). Oct. 5, 1785 Abraham Satterthwaite enters 300 ac in Hyde Co on E side of Pungo R and in the fork of Rusmans Cr; border: James Wilkerson.

316 (7). Oct. 11, 1785 Levi Tuley enters 42 ac in Hyde Co in New Currituck; border: on S side of "the little Gumbs", John Jordan, Thaniel Tuley, William Ester, & with Anthony Tuley's line to the beginning; warrant out.

317 (8). Oct. 17, 1785 Southy Rew jr enters 510 ac in Hyde Co in New Currituck Swamp; border: Solomon Rew, Parker Lacey, & Anthony Tooley's back line; warrant out.

318 (9). Nov. 9, 1785 James Wilkerson enters 100 ac in Hyde Co on E side of Pongo R; border: Stephen Smith esq; warrant out.

page 3
319 (10). Nov. 27, 1785 James Wilkerson enters 300 ac in Hyde Co on E side of Pongo R and W side of Rusmans Cr; border: Antry; warrant out.

320 (11). Nov. 28, 785 George Dukes sr enters 100 ac in Hyde Co on N side of Pongo R and W side of a swamp; warrant out.

321 (12). Dec. 1, 1785 Richard Harvey enters 50 ac in Hyde Co; border: Benjamin Rogers' new entry on W side of Pongo R; warrant out.

322 (13). Dec. 5, 1785 John Lewis sr enters 8,000 ac in Hyde Co; border: Nathaniel Allen, Josiah Collins, Samuel Dickeson, "his" entry No. 10 in Tyrrel [County] Entry Book, along said entries S and W 3 miles, then runs S to Galard's new entry, to the head of Indian Run, down the run to "the Inhabitants lines" of Pongo R, up the river bordering "the Inhabitents", [with] patents lines

of Richard Harvey's new entry, & to the beginning; warrant out for 953 ac and the remainder relapsed for want of purchase money "agreeable to bargin".

page 4
323 (14). Dec. 22, 1785 James Jasper enters 150 ac in Hyde Co on E side of Pongo R and N side of Slade Cr; border: his old line and the back line of Selden Jasper; warrant out.

324 (15). Dec. 22, 1785 Edward McSwain enters 40 ac on Pantigo Swamp; between my "Martin" patent and John Loyd's patent; warrant out.

325 (16). Dec. 22, 1785 Edward McSwain enters 50 ac; in the bounds of Meline's patent; border: Thoms. Galard; warrant out.

326 (17). Jan. 4, 1786 James Wilkerson enters 50 ac in Hyde Co on E side of Pongo R and W side of Wm Russel's line; warrant out.

page 5
327 (18). Jan. 24, 1786 Stephen Smith enters 122 ac in Hyde Co on Mach Pongo R; border: near Dikes' Landing, runs NW 200 poles up "the" River Swamp to John Smith's patent now his own [property], & along Major Clark's patent being now his own; in the cypress swamp called Point Lookout Swamp and the fork of the neck called Heren Run; warrant out.

328 (19). Jan. 24, 1786 James Wilkerson enters 130 ac in Hyde Co on E side of Pongo R; border: Stephen Smith and his own line; warrant out; duplicate issued.

page 6
329 (20). Feb. 21, 1786 Willm Hogges Slade enters 100 ac in Hyde Co on E side of Mch. Pongo R; border: Stephen Smith's SE corner, runs NE with his line to "the" purcoson, with the purcoson to the head of Dips Cr, to a marked cypress Willm Win's corner, with the creek to some small pines in the marsh, & to the beginning; being the land formerly called Nash's land; warrant out; Mar. 4, 1786 caveated by James Wilkerson.

330 (21). Feb. 27, 1786 Zedekiah Swindel 200 ac in Hyde Co on Oter Creeks; between Long shoal R and Matemusket [Lake]; warrant out.

331 (22). Feb. 27, 1786 Samuel Davis enters 50 ac in Hyde Co on N side of Pongo R; border: his old line and Thomas Addams; warrant out.

page 7
332 (23). Feb. 28, 1786 Levy Tuley enters 100 ac in Hyde Co in New Currituck Swamp; border: John Jordan; within "the calls of" Anthony Tuley's patent; warrant out.

333 (24). Mar. 3, 1786 James Wilkerson enters 350 ac in Hyde Co; border: my land, Stephin Smith, & Thomas Addams; warrant out.

334 (25). Mar. 10, 1786 Noah Egleton enters 30 ac in Hyde Co on E side of Pantigo Swamp; border: John Philips and my own line; warrant out.

335 (26). Mar. 15, 1786 Jacob Durden jr enters 50 ac in Hyde Co on E side of Pantigo Cr and W side of Pongo R; warrant out.

page 8
336 (27). Mar. 16, 1786 James Hamilton enters 30 ac in Hyde Co on E side of Pongo R; border: a bay tree corner of James Hamilton's own survey No. 117 [No. 276 above] of 50 ac, runs N15E 60 poles to Slade's old patent, S6E 133 poles with the line of Slade's patent to James Davis' patent, S78E 51 poles along his line to a corner of James Hamilton's survey No 117, & to the beginning; caveated by Capt. Jon Alderson; May 23, 1786 caveat drawn; warrant out.

337 (28). Mar. 27, 1786 Ezekiah Stilley enters 50 ac in Hyde Co on W side of Pongo R; border: Jeremiah Johnson, Willm Davis, Willm Bushop, & between their lines and the river; warrant out.

338 (29). Mar. 27, 1786 Ezekiah Stilley enters 50 ac in Hyde Co on E side of Pongo R; border: James McAbe, the river, & Grassey Ridge; warrant out.

339 (30). Mar. 28, 1786 Christopher Mason enters 50 ac in Hyde Co in New Currituck; border: Solomon Rew, Parker Lacey, & his own line; warrant out.

page 9
340 (31). Mar. 30, 1786 John Aldorson enters 250 ac in Hyde Co on E side of Pungo R and the lower side of Slades Creek mouth; border: Francis Morris, Sanderson's original line, & runs on the river shore to Cedar Cr; warrant out.

341 (32). Mar. 30, 1786 John Aldoson enters 60 ac in Hyde Co; between John Davis' patent and James Hamilon's entry No. 117 [No. 276 above] in Thomas Jordan esq's Entry Office; caveated by Willm Purchase "drawn"; [entry drawn--lined out].

342 (33). May 26, 1786 Simon Larey enters 50 ac in Hyde Co; within "the calls of" Fras Morriss' patent; warrant out.

343 (34). May 29, 1786 James Bray enters 150 ac; border: the head of W prong of Olter Cr, runs S to the head of Little Olter Cr, & W; warrant out.

page 10

344 (35). Jul. 21, 1786 Willm Richd Jasper enters 200 ac in Hyde Co on E side of Masons Bay and S side [at] the head of Rose Bay; includes cypress swamp "chiefly"; warrant out.

345 (36). Jul. 21, 1786 Southy Rew enters 29 ac in Hyde Co in New Currituck and on E side of the head of Jaspers Cr; border: Parker Lacey an said Rew; includes said Rew's pasture; warrant out.

346 (37). Jul. 21, 1786 Parker Lacy enters 11 ac in Hyde Co in New Currituck and on E side of the head of Jaspers Cr; border: Southy Rew's new entry and said Lacy's own land; includes Parker Lacy's pasture; warrant out.

page 11
347 (38). Jul. 21, 1786 William Clark and John Egleton enter 300 ac in Hyde Co on N side of Pamplico R; border: the river shore, runs out to Simon Baley's line, with "the" patents line to the river, & along the river to the beginning; caveated by Thos Jordan; in consequence the purchase drawn; ["entry drawn warrant the same"--lined out].

348 (39). Aug. 10, 1786 William Russell enters 100 ac in Currituck and on S side of Smiths Cr; border: Palmer's patent and Slade; warrant out.

349 (40). Aug. 12, 1786 John Loyd enters 60 ac on S side of Pantigo Cr; border: his own line, Thos Gaylard, & John Egleton; warrant out.

350 (41). Aug. 16,1786 John Tyson enters 600 ac on E side of Pongo R and N side of Broad Cr; border: his own line; warrant out.

page 12
351 (42). Aug. 23,1786 Josiah Jarves enters 122 ac in Hyde Co on N side of Pongo R and E side of Juniper Br; includes said branch, the cypress swamp next [to] the river, & the W branch; warrant out.

352 (43). Aug. 28, 1786 John Egleton enters 96 ac in Hyde Co on N side of Pamlico R; border: runs out from the river to Simon Baley's line and with "the" patent lines to the river; warrant out; "entered in bonnd Book".

Jesse Latham, Entry Taker, appointed May term 1790
353 (1). Jun. 1, 1790 [Andrew Sanders--lined out] enters 50 ac  on E side of Long Shold R; border: on W side of Sand Hills, runs with the S side of "the" point, N to Prince Bay, & with the bay to the beginning; warrant out; [same entry is No. 455 below].

[on cover of next "book"]   Entry Book 1786-1788
page 1

354 (1). Aug. 29, 1786 Jacob Swindell enters 200 ac in Hyde Co between Long Shoal R & Mattamusket [Lake] an at Otter Cr; border: Zedekiah Swindell; warrant.

355 (2). Aug. 29, 1786 Jacob Tuely enters 50 ac in Hyde Co on E side of Jacobs Bay; warrant.

356 (3). Aug. 29, 1786 Enoch Flin enters 100 ac in Hyde Co on N side of Pantigo Mill Pond; border: Benjam. Martin; warrant out.

357 (4). Sept. 30, 1786 Samuel Simpson enters 640 ac in Hyde Co; known as Wades Point; border: Wm Howard, Back Cr, Matchapongo R, & Pamplico R; warrant.

358 (5). Nov. 27, 1786 John Alderson enters 50 ac in Hyde Co; border: McCarty's patent in New Currituck; warrant out.

6. [not in the book; skip in numbers]

page 2
359 (7). Nov. 27, 1786 John Alderson enters 50 ac; border: McCarty's patent in New Currituck; warrant out.

360 (8). Dec. 5, 1786 Simon Alderson enters 357 ac in Hyde Co in New Currituck on E side of Pungo R; border: Thomas Easter, Hezkiah Slade, & John Rees; warrant out.

361 (9). Dec. 17, 1786 Robert Barnet enters 125 ac in Hyde Co on S side of Broad Cr; border: Jaccum, Eborn [or Jaccums Eborn], Benjamin Barnes, William Hollowell, & Robert Barnet; warrant out.

10. [not in the book; skip in numbers]

362 (11). Dec. 19, 1786 Seth Hovey enters 150 ac; border: John Mordrick, Edward Molesley, Archable Holms, & Weeks; warrant out.

363 (12). Dec. 29, 1786 Henry Scott enters 130 ac in Hyde Co on N side of Pungo Cr; border: John Silven, runs with Pungo Cr, & a creek making out of Pungo Cr; caveated Jan. 24, 1787 by Wm Gurganus [warrant out--lined out].

page 3
364 (13). Dec. 29, 1786 Benjamin Russel enters 50 ac in Hyde Co; border: Henry Slade's patent, John Bryan, & near Slades Cr; warrant out.

365 (14). Sept. 29, 1786 [sic] William Russel enters 25 ac in Hyde Co in Currituck; within "the calls of" Benjamin Mason's patent; border: two of William Russel's former patents on Paupau Ridge; warrant out.

366 (15). Jan. 4, 1787 Ephraim Elsbre enters 25 ac in Hyde Co on E side of Pantego Cr; border: John Mandrick's and Benjamin Martin's patents; warrant out.

367 (16). Jan. 4, 1787 Ebenezor Slaide enters 50 ac in Hyde Co runs with Slades Cr to a little creek called Joes Cr; border: John Bryan's and Henry Slade's patents; warrant out.

368 (17). Jan. 8, 1787 Morris Bell enters 30 a in Hyde Co in New Currituck "to" Jaspers Cr, Back Cr, & Long Cr; warrant out.

page 4
369 (18). Jan. 22, 1787 Rubin Bartee enters 368 ac in Hyde Co on E side of Matchapungo R and W side of Silvesters Cr; within "the plott" from the river to [the] back line; caveated Jan. 30, 1786 [sic] by John Aldrson, in consequence, the purch. money drawn "mistake".

370 (19). Jan. 23, 1787 Simond Alderson enters 22 ac in Hyde Co on E side of Matchapungo R; border: a new survey of James Hamilton decd, Wm Banks, & James Fortescue; warrant out.

371 (20). Jan. 23, 1787 Rubin Bartee enters 500 ac in Hyde Co in New Currituck, near Smiths Cr, & Pungo R; between John Smith and Richard Jordan; Mar. 26, 1787 caveated by Elizebeth Silvester, purchase money drawn.

372 (21). Jan. 24, 1787 John Allen and John Loyd enter 640 ac in Hyde Co on SW side of Pantigo Cr; border: Thomas Gaylard, John Gaylard, Noah Egleton, John Egleton, & John Loyhad; includes the land between the lines and Pantego Cr; warrant out.

page 5
373 (22). Jan. 28, 1787 Thomas Smith enters 80 ac in Hyde Co on E side of Pungo R and at the mouth of Silvesters Cr; border: said creek and Charles Smith's patent; Feb. 27, 1787 caveated by William Russel.

374 (23). Feb. 2, 1787 Ephrim Elsbre enters 200 ac on Silvesters Cr; border: Thomas Smith's late entry, runs up the creek to Charles Smith's line, to Thomas Smith's new entry, & with said entry to the creek; Feb. 27, 1787 caveated by William Russel, purchase money drawn.

# Hyde County, NC Land Entries 1778-1795

375 (24). Feb. 2, 1787 John Allen enters 200 ac in Hyde Co in Pantego Swamp and Mill "Pound"; between Benjamin Martin's patent and runs up the swamp; warrant out.

376 (25). Feb. 2,1787 Ruben Bartee enters 500 ac on E side of Matchapungo R and lower side of Silvesters Cr; border: said river and creek; Mar. 26, 1787 caveated by Elizebeth Silvester, purchase money drawn.

page 6
377 (26). Feb. 10, 1787 Henry Levenworth enters 150 ac in Hyde Co on SW side of Pantigo Cr; border: Edward McSwain and Cambell; warrant.

378 (27). Feb. 21, 1787 Thomas Gaylard enters 100 ac in Hyde Co on N side of Broad Creek Swamp; border: Chinkepine Nole; warrant.

379 (28). Feb. 21, 1787 John Allen and Thomas Blackledge enter 640 ac in Hyde Co between Pamplico R and Machapungo R; being the land called Wades Point; includes the vacant land between said point and Baily's line.

380 (29). Feb. 21, 1787 John Allen enters 320 ac in Hyde Co on E side of Machpungo R; warrant.

381 (30). Feb. 21, 1787 John Allen enters 320 ac in Hyde Co on E side of Machapungo R; warrant.

382 (31). Feb. 21, 1787 John Allen enters 300 ac in Hyde Co on E side of Machapungo R; warrant.

page 7
383 (32). Feb. 21, 1787 John Allen enters 400 ac in Hyde Co on W side of Machapungo R; warrant.

384 (33). Feb. 21, 1787 John Allen enters 200 ac in Hyde Co on E side of Machapungo R; warrant.

385 (34). Feb. 21, 1787 John Allen enters 160 ac in Hyde Co on W side of Machapungo R; warrant.

386 (35). Feb. 21, 1787 John Allen enters 160 ac in Hyde Co on W side of Machapungo R; warrant.

387 (36). Feb. 26, 1787 Ann Banks enters 159 ac in Hyde Co on E side of Machapungo R, S side of "Slads" Cr, & W side of Dunkin Cr; border: Robert Banks and Ash Cr; warrant.

388 (37). Feb. 27, 1787 William Russel enters 25 ac in Hyde Co in New Currituck; between his Great Ridge patent and "his patent" on E side of "said" patent; warrant.

page 8
389 (38). Mar. 10, 1787 Simon Alderson enters 140 ac in Hyde Co on E side of Machapungo R and on S side of Slade Cr.

390 (39). Mar. 12, 1787 Leavy Tuely enters 250 ac in Hyde Co on E side of Masons Bay; border: the mouth of Broad Cr on S side, runs along Rush point Cove to the bay, with the bay to "the uper" Island Point, & up Uper Island Cr; includes the surplus land in bounds of Jeremiah Tuely's patent.

391 (40). [no date] Ebenezor Juell enters 120 ac in Hyde Co on the head of Ducking Cr and in New Currituck on E side of Machapungo R; border: runs with the creek to John Slade's line, with the line far enough to includes 120 ac, down to Slades Cr, & down said creek to the beginning.

392 (41). Mar. 13, 1787 William Cording enters 50 ac in Hyde Co "up" Pungo Cr; border: Church Windly's line and runs down "towards" the bridge.

393 (42). Mar. 22, 1787 Mikell Windley enters 100 ac on N side of Pungo R; border: said Mikell Windley's line, James Eborn, & Pungo Cr.

page 9
394 (43). Mar. 24, 1787 Ruben Slade enters 200 ac in Hyde Co on W side of Machapungo R and N side of Pantigo Cr; border: Columb. Flinn's Jacks Neck patent; warrant.

395 (44). Mar. 26, 1787 John Jordan enters 100 ac in Hyde Co; warrant.

396 (45). Mar. 29, 1787 James Mickins enters 30 ac in Hyde Co on E side of Machapungo R at John Slade's beginning [corner]; border: runs along John Slade's line far enough to include 30 ac, down to Slades Cr, & with the creek to the beginning; warrant.

397 (46). Apr. 13, 1787 Jacob Wilkerson enters 100 ac in Hyde Co on NE side of Broad Cr; border: my third line at Broad Cr, runs N30W with my line to Thomas Gaylard's line, & with his line to Broad Cr.

page 10
398 (47). Apr. 15, 1787 Isaack Wilkerson enters 100 ac in Hyde Co on N side of Pantego Cr; border: Littleton Eborn and Isaack Wilkerson's back line; warrant.

399 (48). Apr. 15, 1787 Thomas Baily enters 200 ac in Hyde Co; border: his "oald" shop landing at the head of Writes Cr; warrant.

400 (49). Apr. 15, 1787 Simon Baily enters 100 ac in Hyde Co on N side of Pamplico R; border: near John Far's Gutt; warrant out.

401 (50). Apr. 29, 1787 William Wright enters 200 ac in Hyde Co on W side of Machapungo R and in the fork of Oeshter Cr; border: the head of the "oald" bridge; warrant out.

402 (51). Apr. 29, 1787 John Wright enters 100 ac in Hyde Co on W side of Machapungo R; border: Williams William Wright's [sic] late [written over "new"] entry; warrant out.

page 11
403 (52). May 1, 1787 James Eborn enters 50 ac in Hyde Co on N side of Pungo Cr and runs down the creek; border: said James [Eborn] and Michael Windley's upper corner; warrant out.

404 (53). May 28, 1787 Bethuell Baily enters 50 ac in Hyde Co on W side of Machapungo R; includes the vacant land between S line of his "old plantation" and the river; warrant out.

405 (54). May 28, 1787 Seth Cipps enters 250 ac in Hyde Co on W side of Matchapungo R and W side of N Dividing Cr; warrant out.

406 (55). May 28, 1787 Thomas Gaylard enters 100 ac in Hyde Co on W side of Pantego Cr; border: John Gaylard, Johnathan Gerganous, & Thomas Gaylard; warrant out.

407 (56). May 29, 1787 Isaack Wilkerson enters 50 ac in Hyde Co on N side of Pantigo Cr on N side & head of Ingoes Cr and W side of Pungo R.

page 12
408 (57). May 30, 1787 John Allen enters 300 ac in Hyde Co on E side of Matchapungo R; within the "supposed" lines of Charles Smith's patent; between Smiths Cr and Broad Cr; warrant out.

409 (58). Jun. 11, 1787 Jerimiah Johnson enters 100 ac in Hyde Co on W side of Pungo R and S side of Indian Run; border: Jacob Paul; warrant out.
410 (59). Jun. 21, 1787 Seth Hovey and Ephm Elsbre enter 300 ac in Hyde Co on W side of Matchapungo R and in the Great Savanah Devil Woodyard; border: Seth Hovey's former entry No. 11 [No. 362 above] made in said Elsbre's Office, Mosley, & Archable Homesley; warrant out.

411 (60). Jul. 3, 1787 John Mollerson enters 50 ac on W side of N Dividing Cr; border: Joseph Eckol; warrant out.

page 13
412 (61). Jul. 14, 1787 William Banks enters 25 ac in Hyde Co on E side of Matchapungo R and S side of Slades Cr; border: Ann Banks, Slades Cr, my own line, John Davis, & James "Hammilton"; warrant out.

413 (62). Jul. 18, 1787 Abram Jordan enters 150 ac in Hyde Co on W side of Pungo R; border: James Webster and Thomas Jordan; warrant out.

414 (63). Jul. 21, 1787 Vallentine Jasper enters 150 ac in Hyde Co on N side of Slades Cr and E side of Pungo R; border: a red oak corner of Thomas Smith's patent now property of James Jasper, runs N26W 240 poles, then to Daniel Tyson's corner pine, & to the beginning; Sept. 30, 1787 caveated by James Jasper, the purchase money drawn.

415 (64). Jul. 29, 1787 Jesse Allen enters 90 ac in Hyde Co on E side of Pungo R and N side of Slades Cr; border: Benjamin Cleaves's "old" survey.

page 14
416 (65). Jul. 30, 1787 Vallentine Jasper enters 38 ac in Hyde Co on N side of Slades Cr and E side of Pungo R; border: a red oak corner of Thomas Smith's patent now the property of James Jasper, runs N26W 240 poles to a supposed corner of Thos Smith's patent, N87W to Matthias Tyson's NE corner pine, & to the beginning; Sept. 30, 1787 caveated by James Jasper, the purchase money drawn.

417 (66). Aug. 10, 1787 Zacheriah Tyson enters 150 ac in Hyde Co on E side of Pungo R and N side of Slades Cr; border: the mouth of a small creek making out of Collins Cr, runs to Matthias Tyson's corner pine, S12E to Tysons Cr, down Tysons Cr to Slades Cr, & to the beginning; warrant out.

418 (67). Aug. 19, 1787 John Allen enters 150 ac in Hyde Co on S side of Pungo Cr and W side of Jacks Cr.

419 (68). Aug. 22, 1787 James Jasper enters 162 ac in Hyde Co on E side of Pungo R and N side of Slades Cr; border: a pine proved to be Matthias Tyson's NE corner, runs S11¼ E to Slades Cr near Jonathan Jasper's Shipyard, down the creek to Tysons Cr, up Tysons Cr to its head, & to the beginning; warrant out.

page 15
420 (69). Sept. 2, 1787 Richard Harvey enters 50 ac in Hyde Co on W side of Pungo R; border: Stephen Smith, Joshua Smith, & Thos McWilliams; warrant out.

421 (70). Sept. 14, 1787 John Abrams enters 100 ac in Hyde Co on W side of Pungo R and at the head of the main branch of N Dividing Cr; warrant out.

422 (71). Sept. 20, 1787 Zacheriah Barrow enters 100 ac in Hyde Co on W side of Pungo R; border: his own line; warrant out.

423 (72). Nov. 10, 1787 Ephm Elsbre enters 150 ac in Hyde Co on N side of Pungo R; border: near Grass Ridge Gutt and runs down the river; warrant out.

424 (73). Nov. 19, 1787 John Allen enters 200 ac in Hyde Co on W side of Matchapungo R and S side of Pungo Cr; border: B H Silby's patent "that" joins Barrow's patent on Pungo Cr; warrant out.

425 (74). Dec. 3, 1787 Jesse Noah Baily enters 80 ac in Hyde Co on W side of N Dividing Cr; border: Seth Cipps; warrant out.

page 16
426 (75). Dec. 31, 1787 John Winfield sr enters 60 ac in Hyde Co on W side of Pungo R; border: my own "oald" & new lines and the Beach Ridge patent; warrant out.

427 (76). Dec. 31, 1787 Henry Germain enters 150 ac in Hyde Co on W side of Pungo R; border: John Winfield sr and Simon Bright in Jacks Neck; warrant out.

428 (77). Feb. 12, 1788 John Egleton enters 60 ac in Hyde Co on E side of Pungo R; border: Solleman Smith and Josiah Jarvis; warrant out.

429 (78). Feb. 12, 1788 John Egleton enters 60 ac in Hyde Co on W side of Pungo R; border: Mordrick and Seth Fortescue; warrant out.

430 (79). Feb. 13, 1788 James Wilkerson enters 200 ac in Hyde Co on E side of Pungo R and W side of Cupton's Cr; border: his own survey; warrant out.

page 17
431 (80). Feb. 13, 1788 James Wilkerson enters 200 ac in Hyde Co on W side of Pungo R; border: Joseph Curtis and John Davis; warrant out.

432 (81). Mar. 5, 1788 Joseph Leach enters 450 ac on N side of Pungo R; border: on the front of his own land called the Bay patent and below Satterthwaite; warrant out.

433 (82). Mar. 6, 1788 Jesse Noah Baily enters 80 ac in Hyde Co on W side of Pungo R, on N side of Pamplico R, & W side of N Dividing Cr; border: his own entry No. 74 [No. 425 above] [made] in Ephm Elsbre's Entry Office; warrant out.

434 (83). Mar. 6, 1788 Ephm Elsbre enters 150 ac in Hyde Co on W side of N Dividing Cr; border: Jesse Noah Baily's late entry and the creek; warrant out.

435 (84). Mar. 24, 1788 Joses [or Josep] Eckols enters 70 ac in Hyde Co on N side of Pamplico R; border: Boass Hammond, Holems Pairtree, & the river; warrant out.

436 (85). Mar. 26, 1788 John Fortescue sr enters 30 ac on E side of Pungo R and S side of "Slaes" Cr; border: Samuel Slade, Richard Booty, Richard Ballance, & Samuel Fortescue; warrant out.

page 18
437 (86). Mar. 29, 1788 Joses Eckols enters 20 ac in Hyde Co; within the bounds of Holms pasutre patent; being the surplus [land] between Pamplico R and his back line; warrant out.

438 (87). Mar. 29, 1788 Jesse Allen enters 110 ac in Hyde Co on E side of Pungo R in New Currituck; border: his own entry; warrant out.

439 (88). Apr. 16, 1788 Samuel Slade enters 300 ac in Hyde Co on E side of Pungo R and N side of Shallop Cr; border: Samuel Davis; warrant out.

440 (89). Apr. 21, 1788 James Robins enters 200 ac in Hyde Co on W side of Pungo R; Jun. 10, 1788 caveated by James Webster.

441 (90). Apr. 30, 1788 George Barrow enters 50 ac on W side of Pungo Cr; between said creek & David Perkins' line and runs up the creek & swamp "as the branch" that parts my land from Zaceriah Barrow's land; warrant out.

442 (91). Apr. 30, 1788 Burage Huchen Silby enters 100 ac in Hyde Co; border: said Silby's West corner of a patent late the property of Benjamin Martin, runs with said patent to "the" savanah "the S corner being Hosea Martin's", & with said Martin's line to the beginning; this entry caveated, the money drawn ["warrant out"--lined out].

page 19
443 (92). Apr. 30, 1788 Burage Huchen Silby enters 340 ac in Hyde Co on W side of Pungo R; border: near the mouth of a small gutt on Pungo R and runs with the former "oald" line "all ready laid out" for Benjamin Martin "Dect" and Rotheous Latham purchased of "one" Brite; this entry caveated, and money drawn.

444 (93). Apr. 30, 1788 Burage Huchen Silby enters 75 ac in Hyde Co on W side of Pungo R; border: William Daw "Dect" line on Brites Cr, runs S, & W to the beginning; this entry caveated, the money drawn.

445 (94). May 27, 1788 William Watson enters 50 ac in Hyde Co on S side of the lake; border: Wm Watson sr's E corner, with said Watson's line to Caleb Swindal, & with "said" line to Isarel Watson's line; warrant out.

446 (95). May 27, 1788 Rebecca Tycon enters 114 ac in Hyde Co on W side of Pungo R; border: a marked sweet gum at the mouth of Canoe Br, runs up the swamp 98 poles to Saml Davis' beginning black gum in Ash Br, along his line "25" to the main "rhoade", along Danl Tycon's line to a black gum the division corner between Elizabeth Wiley, Rd Smith, Thos McWilliams, & with the branch to the beginning.

page 20
447 (96). May 28, 1788 Joseph English enters 150 ac in Hyde Co on Juniper Bay; between Augustin Spain and Josiah Jervis on the head of Will Cr; warrant out.

448 (97). Jun. 13, 1788 John Satchwell enters 100 ac on E side of Pungo R; border: Benjamin Rogers; includes the "plantation" and cultivated land; at a place known as the Elbow on the river; warrant out.

449 (98). Jul. 1, 1788 Jesse Latham enters 77 ac in Hyde Co on W side of Pungo R; border: the land left [to] me by my father; warrant out.

450 (99). Jul. 21, 1788 Thos Wright enters 50 ac in Hyde Co on W side of Pungo R; border: James Jordan and James Bachlor; warrant out.

451 (100). Sept. 6, 1778 Benjamin Parmelee enters 100 ac in Hyde Co on E side of Pungo R and E side of Slades Cr; between said creek and Samuel Slade's "dect" patent; warrant out.

452 (101). Oct. 6, 1788 Holms Pairtree enters 57.5 ac in Hyde Co on N side of Pamplico R and W side of N Dividing Cr; border: on S side of Seth Cipps' line and joins his own land; warrant out.

page 21
453 (102). Feb. 24, 1788 [sic] Henry Scott enters 100a c in Hyde Co on W side of Pungo R; warrant out.
454 (103). Feb. 25, 1788 [sic] Seth Windley enters 100 ac in Hyde Co on E side of Pungo Swamp; border: Roger Jones' patent, Maple Windley's patent, & runs in the Back Dismal [Swamp]; known as Holly Ridge; warrant out.

page 22   [blank page]

[The remainder of the entries are in SS 955.4.]
page 1
455 (1). Jun. 1, 1790 Andrew Sanders enters 50 ac in Hyde Co on E side of Long Shoal R and on W side of the Sand Hills; border: runs with the S side of "the" point, runs S to Price Bay, & with the bay to the beginning; warrant issued.

456 (2). Jun. 1, 1790 William Watson enters 60 ac in Hyde Co on S side of Mattamuskeet Lake; border: the lake, Weston's line on E, Samuel Silby's patent on W, Silby's beginning corner on the lake, runs down the lake to Weston's line, S with Weston's line, W, & N to the beginning; warrant issued.

457 (3). Jun. 1, 1790 Elliott Clayton enters 106 ac in Hyde Co [on] E end of Mattamuskeet Lake; being the surplus land in James Clayton's patent; warrant.

458 (4). Jun. 2, 1790 Thomas Gibbs sr enters 20 ac in Hyde Co on S side of Mattamuskeet Lake; between his own line & the lake and runs "up" the lake; warrant.

page 2
459 (5). Jun. 2, 1790 Abel Hutson enters 70 ac in Hyde Co on E side of Pungo R; border: William Fortescue's E corner at a poplar, runs with said line to "the" creek, with the "Boey" to John Taley's line, to Francis Crudler's line, & to the beginning; warrant.

460 (6). Jun. 8, 1790 Joseph Smith enters 100 ac in Hyde Co on E side of Pungo Cr; border: Caleb Toreman, Benjamin Toreman, & between them and Scott; warrant.

461 (7). Jul. 5, 1790 John Jordan sr enters 50 ac in Hyde Co on N side of Mattamuskeet Lake; border: his own land; warrant.

462 (8). Jan. 16, 1791 Samuel Weston enters 35 ac in Hyde Co on S side of Matamuskeet Lake; border: the upper corner of Thomas Gibbs' new entry; warrant.

page 3
463 (9). Jan. 17, 1791 John Wood enters 100 ac in Hyde Co near a small "noal" and near Murpheys Savannah; border: runs to Seth Windly's line, Murphy's Savannah, & to the beginning; warrant issued.

464 (10). Jan. 18, 1791 Benjamin Bamey enters 100 ac in Hyde Co on N side of Pungo Cr; border: Sullivan's patent at "his" beginning, runs S down "the" creek to Pungo Cr, along Pungo Cr to where Sullivan's line "strikes the water", & along his line to the beginning; warrant issued.

465 (11). Feb. 9, 1791 Henry Scott enters 60 ac in Hyde Co on N side of Pungo Cr; between Benjamin Bemey, William Howard, & William Genganas; warrant.

466 (12). Feb. 12, 1791 John Bray enters 200 ac between Mattamuskeet [Lake] and Long Shoal R; warrant.

apge 4

467 (13). Feb. 12, 1791 William Harris sr enters 19 ac; between John Cooprs & [John--lined out] Gibbs' "long" patent and joins Claton's line; warrant.

468 (14). Mar. 14, 1791 John Sadler enters 640 ac on Swan Quarter [Bay]; border: Francis Crudle; warrant.

469 (15). Mar. 14, 1791 David Green enters 110 ac on Swan Quarter [Bay]; warrant

470 (16). Mar. 15, 1791 Ebenezer Jester enters 200 ac in Hyde Co near Capps Cr; border: W of William Williams, Nathan Selby, & Solomon Jones; warrant.

471 (17). Mar. 25, 1791 Joseph Picquet enters 200 ac in Hyde Co on Swan Quarter [Bay]; between Alyaslus Span & John Sadler and joins Josiah Jones; warrant.

page 5

472 (18). Apr. 21, 1791 Shadrack Windly enters 50 ac in Hyde Co on N side of Pungo Cr; between Henry Scott jr and William Howard; warrant out.

473 (19). May 23, 1791 Joseph Picque enters 600 ac on Swan Quarter [Bay]; border: behind Josiah Jarvis, John Sadler, William Carrawan, & runs to "the" savannah next to "the" lake; warrant out.

474 (20). May 24, 1791 Jacob Swindell enters 90 ac in Hyde Co on Otters Cr; between Mattamuskeet [Lake] and Long Shoal R; border: Ezekiah Swindell's beginning and John Bray; warrant out.

475 (21). May 30, 1791 Elliot Clayton enters 100 ac on E side of Mattamuskeet Lake; border: Elliot's former line, Gills' line, & runs West; warrant issued.

page 6

476 (22). Jun. 11, 1791 Henry Tooley enters 150 ac on Great Judas Island; warrant out.

477 (23). Aug. 9, 1791 Stephen Gaylard enters 200 ac in Hyde Co on W side of Pungo R; border: near E side of Benjamin Gaylard's patent; warrant out.

478 (24). Aug. 30, 1791 John Bray sr enters 200 ac on Mattamuskeet Lake; border: his own patent; warrant issued.

479 (25). Sept. 22, 1791 William Cohoon enters 35 ac on Mattamuskeet Lake Swamp; border: Petres' line, Gibbs' old patent, Swindell, & Col. Leach; warrant issued.

page 7

480 (26). Nov. 28, 1791 James Hodges enters 8 ac in Hyde Co on S side of Mattamuskeet Lake; between William Carrowin, Silby, & the lake; warrant issued.

481 (27). Nov. 29, 1791 Josiah Jarvis enters 640 ac on E side of Swan Quarter [Bay] next to Juniper Bay; within the lines of said Josiah Jarvis and back of "them"; warrant issued.

482 (28). Nov. 29, 1791 William Harris esq enters 100 ac on Mattamuskeet [Lake]; border: Gibbs' "long" patent and Gen. Armstrong's NW corner formerly Hugh Henry's line; warrant issued.

483 (29). Dec. 5, 1791 Joseph Smith enters 30 ac on N side of Pungo Cr; border: his own land; warrant issued.

page 8
484 (30). Dec. 24, 1791 Henry Scott enters 30 ac in Hyde Co on N side of Pungo Cr; between Shadrack Windly, Henry Scott jr, & Samuel Manduel; warrant issued.

485 (31). Dec. 24, 1791 Henry Scott enters 100 ac in Hyde Co on N side of Pungo Cr; between Joseph Smith, William Howard, Henry Scott jr, & Foreman; warrant issued.

486 (32). Jan. 26, 1792 Thomas Cording enters 50 ac; between Hancock and Joseph Cording; warrant issued.

487 (33). Feb. 28, 1792 Zachariah Jarvis enters 75 ac in Hyde Co on Swan Quarter [Bay]; being surplus land in Benjamin Mason's patent; warrant issued.

488 (34). Feb. 28, 1792 Thomas English enters 100 ac on Juniper Cr; between William Turner and Noans Cr; warrant issued.

page 9
489 (35). Mar. 8, 1792 James Eborn enters 100 ac on N side of Pungo Cr; border: said Eborn's corner; warrant.

490 (36). Apr. 1, 1792 James Smith enters 50 ac on N side of Pungo Cr; border: Henry Scott jr, William Howard sr, & his own line; warrant.

page 10   [blank page]

page 11
491 (37). Apr. 24, 1792 Henry Clark enters 150 ac on N side of Pungo R; in the bounds of Jones' patent and near the head of Dowry Cr; border: NW corner of said patent being the "local" land; warrant issued.

492 (38). May 22, 1792 Patrick Williams enters 50 ac in Hyde Co on W side of Pungo R; border: the land formerly called Leath's; warrant issued.

493 (39). May 27, 1792 John Benson enters 100 ac on Mattamuskeet [Lake]; border: James English and William Albert sr; warrant issued.

494 (40). May 27, 1792 John Benson enters 50 ac in Hyde Co on Southwest Bay; border: back of Salathul Lary and on Juniper Bay; warrant issued.

page 12
495 (41). Aug. 4, 1792 William Cohoon enters 22 ac in Hyde Co on Mattamuskeet [Lake]; border: on W side of Josiah Swindell, on Huches line, & his own former entry; warrant issued.

496 (42). Aug. 8, 1792 Thomas Smith enters 220 ac; being surplus lands in "his own" bounds of Charles Smith's patent; said patent borders: Sylvesters Cr, Smiths Cr, & on Match a Pungo R [sic]; warrant issued.

497 (43). Oct. 23, 1792 Thomas Tuley sr enters 200 ac in Hyde Co on E side of the head of Rose Bay; border: a marked cypress in "the" porcoson, runs E, & "so round" to the beginning; inclues 500 [sic] ac; warrant issued.

498 (44). Oct. 26, 1792 Edward Simmons enters 100 ac in Hyde Co "up" Pantego Mill Pond; border: Benjamin Hollowell's patent; warrant issued.

page 13
499 (45). Oct. 26, 1792 Isaac Wilkinson enters 100 ac in Hyde Co on W side of Pungo R and runs up Pantego Mill Pond; border: Edward Simmons' patent [sic] made the same day; warrant issued.

500 (46). Nov. 13, 1792 Archibald McCarty enters 60 ac in Currituck; border: Thomas Easter and Solomon Rew; warrant issued.

501 (47). Nov. 15, 1792 James Dunbar enters 300 ac in Hyde Co on Juniper Swamp; between the head of Long Shaol R and Alligator R; warrant issued.

502 (48). Nov. 30, 1792 Henry Silby and Jesse Latham enter 400 ac in Hyde Co on N side of Mattamuskeet Lake; border: back of Porter's place, near William Daily, & between the lake and "the" new land; warrant issued.

503 (49). Dec. 4, 1792 Thomas Mallison enters 50 ac in Hyde Co; border: John Mallison and between "the" hiding oak & Esther Thoreogeoas; warrant issued.

page 14

504 (50). Dec. 4, 1792 Thomas Mallison enters 80 ac in Hyde Co on N Dividing Cr; between Cox, Seth Fortescue, & John Chambers sr; warrant issued.

505 (51). Dec. 8, 1792 James Hall enters 100 ac on E side of Mattamusket Lake; border: Elliot Clayton's corner along the lake; warrant issued.

506 (52). Dec. 21, 1792 Fredrick Rew enters 50 ac in Hyde Co on E side of Pungo R in new Currituck; border: Mark Rew's patent and Thomas Clark; warrant issued.

"End of the year at 1792"

page 15   "Jan. 1, 1793"
507 (53). Jan. 8, 1793 Archibald McCarty enters 25 ac; border: his own land and John Aldorson; warrant issued.

508 (54). Jan. 8, 1793 John Farrow enters 300 ac on Mount Pleasant; border: S end of his patent, W of his land, & joins Peter Serman; warrant issued.

509 (55). Jan. 8, 1793 Hezekiah Farrow, of Currituck Co, enters 100 ac in Hyde Co on E side of Horon Bay; border: the back line of Clayton's patent; warrant issued.

510 (56). Jan. 10, 1793 Abel Hutson enters 50 ac on E side of Swan Quarter Bay; between Thomas Mason, Francis Crudle, & Foster Jarvis; warrant issued.

page 16
511 (57). Jan. 21, 1793 Benjamin Russel enters 50 ac on E side of Pungo R in New Currituck Swamp; border: Charles Smith's patent that Thomas Smith now possessed, his own patent he purchased of Len Palmer, & Charles Smith's patent at a division line between William Russel and Benjamin Russel; warrant issued.

512 (58). Feb. 14, 1793 John Eborn enters 30 ac in Hyde Co on S side of Pungo Cr; border: Fredrick Foreman anad Peter Harris; warrant issued.

513 (59). Feb. 23, 1793 Benjamin Gibbs jr and Thomas Gibbs jr enter 600 ac in Hyde Co on N side of Wappaping Cr; border: back line of the land in possession of heirs of John Smith sr decd; warrant issued.

514 (60). Feb. 25, 1793 Ezekiel Harris enters 100 ac on E end of Mattamuskeet Lake; border: James Clayton and the place called the Coves; warrant issued.

page 17
515 (61). Feb. 25, 1793 Isaiah Harris enters 100 ac in Hyde Co; border: "partly on" Clayton and Gibbs formerly William Palner's on Mattamuskeet Lake; the place called the Flatts; warrant issued.

516 (62). Feb. 25, 1793 Samuel Henry enters 126 ac in Hyde Co on N side of Wappapping Cr; being the surplus in James Daccson's patent; warrant issued.

517 (63). Feb. 25, 1793 James Mason enters 150 ac in Hyde Co on W end of Mattamuskeet Lake; warrant issued.

518 (64). Feb. 26, 1793 John Bray sr enters 200 ac in Hyde Co between Mattamuskeet [Lake] and Long Shoal R; warrant issued.

519 (65). Feb. 26, 1793 Joseph Sinnon enters 100 ac in Hyde Co on S side of Mattamuskeet Lake; border: Samuel Selby's back line, Abraham Jones, & John Eborn; warrant issued.

page 18
520 (66). Feb. 26, 1793 William Watson enters 8 ac on S side of Mattamuskeet [Lake]; border: runs from a poplar on Swindell's line to Israel Watson's line, with Israel Watson's line to Wm Watson's line, & to the beginning; warrant issued.

521 (67). Mar. 23, 1793 Thomas Smith 130 ac; in the bounds of Charles Smith's patent; border: a former entry made by said Smith; warrant issued.

522 (68). May 13, 1793 Peter Spady enters 50 ac on N side of Pungo R; border: near E end of Stephen Gaylard's patent; known as Keepers Island; warrant issued.

523 (69). May 13, 1793 Peter Spady enters 50 ac on N side of Pungo R; border: W of Richard Harvey's patent; known as Stamping Ridges; warrant issued.

page 19
524 (70). May 28, 1793 William Booty enters 6 ac in Hyde Co on E side of Pungo R in Currituck; border: D Mecarty, Samuel Slade, & William Davis; warrant issued.

525 (71). Jun. 5, 1793 Benjamin Rogers enters 100 ac on E side of Pungo R; border: Solomon Smith's corner, runs NE with his line to Richard Harvey's line, with his line to the River Swamp, & to the beginning; warrant issued.

526 (72). Jul. 27, 1793 John Chambers enters 40 ac; border: John Abram, Seth Fortescue, Caleb Foreman, & Lazarus Foreman; warrant issued.

527 (73). Aug. 2, 1793 William Hollowell enters 100 ac in Hyde Co on N side of Pungo R; border: Solomon Smith's beginning, runs N with Smith's line, to the river, & to the beginning; warrant issued.

page 20
528 (74). Aug. 28, 1793 James Hall enters 15 ac on Mattamuskeet Lake Flats; border: the upper end of his former patent; warrant issued.

529 (75). Aug. 28, 1793 John Mason enters 150 ac; border: the first corner of John Mason's patent granted in 1723/4, runs NE to "the" porcoson, "towards" head of Rose Bay, down to Thomas Mason's back line, along his line to John Mason's back line, & with his line to the beginning; warrant issued.

530 (76). Sep. 7, 1793 Jesse Davis enters 50 ac on E side of Pungo R; border: the Bed of Reeds; warrant issued.

531 (77). Sept. 7, 1793 John Davis jr enters 50 ac on E side of Pungo R; border: on E side of Rotheas Latham's survey; warrant issued.

532 (78). Sept. 7, 1793 John Davis jr enters 50 ac on W side of Pungo R; border: on Juniper Br on Janus Jones' line; warrant issued.

page 21
533 (79). Sept. 7, 1793 William Clayton 150 ac in Hyde Co on Mattamuskeet Lake; border: Porter and James Clayton "300 ac pats"; warrant issued.

534 (80). Sept. 28, 1793 William Clark enters 100 ac in Hyde Co "up" Pungo R; border: near Richard Harvey's entry; warrant issued.

535 (81). Oct. 1, 1793 Jasper Keach enters 150 ac in Hyde Co on S side of Pungo Cr; border: his own line near Piney Savanah, Thomas Aldorson, "to" said Keach's upper survey, & "round"; warrant issued.

536 (82). Oct. 14, 1793 John Davis sr enters 50 ac on W side of Pungo R and on Indian Run; border: near Jacob Paul's beginning and "so round"; warrant issued.

page 22
537 (83). Nov. 20, 1793 Henry Selby enters 640 ac on Mattamuskeet [Lake]; border: his own land patented by John M Harvey, William Pyott, on Malberry Ridge, & S and W of Wysoching Cr; warrant issued.

538 (84). Nov. 26, 1793 Reuben Benson and John Benson enter 60 ac on Mattamuskeet [Lake]; border: Caleb Whetor's corner on the lake and runs upwards; warrant issued.

539 (85). Nov. 26, 1793 Cason Gibbs enters 100 ac on Cypress Swamp on S side of Mattamuskeet Lake; border: near Samuel Weston; warrant issued.

540 (86). Nov. 26, 1793 Cason Gibbs enters 50 ac on swmp land near Southwest Bay; warrant issued.

page 23
541 (87). Nov. 26, 1793 William Porter jr enters 125 ac on N side of Mattamuskeet Lake; border: on NW side of said Porter's land; warrant issued.

542 (88). Nov. 26, 1793 Isaiah Harris enters 50 ac on Mattamuskeet Lake Flats; border: Ezekiel Harris sr's corner and "so round"; warrant issued.

543 (89). Dec. 14, 1793 William Clark enters 400 ac on W side of Pungo R; border: Richard Harvey sr, Jonathan Saterthwaite, & Richard Harvey jr; warrant issued.

544 (90). Dec. 27, 1793 Jacob Darden enters 600 ac on W side of Pungo R and above Indian Run; border: back of Hezekiah Stilley's land in a juniper swamp; warrant issued.

"End of the year 1793"

page 24    "Jan. 1, 1794"
545 (91). Feb. 11, 1794 John G Blount enters 640 ac; border: where Collins and Company's land leaves the patent land on Pungo R and runs to the back of "the" lines down the river; warrant issued.

546 (92). Feb. 11, 1794 John G Blount enters 640 ac; border: his own entry No. 91 and the patent lines down Pungo R; warrant issued.

547 (93). Feb. 11, 1794 John G Blount enters 640 ac; border: entry No. 92 and the patent lines down Pungo R; warrant issued.

548 (94). Feb. 11, 1794 John G Blount enters 640 ac; border: entry No. 93 and the patent lines down Pungo R; warrant issued.

549 (95). Feb. 11, 1794 John G Blount enters 640 ac in Hyde Co; border: entry No. 94 and the patent lines down Pungo R; warrant issued.

page 25
550 (96). Feb. 11, 1794 John G Blount enters 640 ac; border: his entry No. 95 and the patent lines down Pungo R; warrant issued.

551 (97). Feb. 11, 1794 John G Blount enters 640 ac; border: his entry No. 96 and the patent lines down Pungo R; warrant issued.

552 (98). Feb. 11, 1794 John G Blount enters 640 ac; border: entry No. 97 and the patent lines down Pungo R; warrant issued.

553 (99). Feb. 11, 1794 John G Blount enters 640 ac; border: entry No. 98 and the patent lines down Pungo R; warrant issued.

554 (100). Feb. 11, 1794 John G Blount enters 640 ac; border: entry No. 99 and the patent lines down Pungo R; warrant issued.

555 (101). Feb. 11, 1794 John G Blount enters 640 ac; border: entry No. 100 and the patent lines down Pungo R; warrant issued.

page 26
556 (102). Feb. 11, 1794 John G Blount enters 640 ac; border: his entry No. 101 and the patent lines down Pungo R; "w".

557 (103). Feb. 11, 1794 John G Blount enters 640 ac; border: his entry No. 102, the patent lines down Pungo R, & runs S and E; "w".

558 (104). Feb. 11, 1794 John G Blount enters 640 ac; border: his entry No. 103, the patent lines down Pungo R, & runs S; "w".

559 (105). Feb. 11, 1794 John G Blount enters 640 ac; border: his entry No. 105, the old patent lines, & runs S and E; "w".

106. [skip in numbers; not in the book]

560 (107). Feb. 11, 1794 John G Blount enters 640 ac; border: his entry No. 106; "w".

561 (108). Feb. 11, 1794 John G Blount enters 640 ac in Hyde Co; border: his entry No. 107; "w".

page 27
562 (109). Feb. 11, 1794 John G Blount enters 640 ac; border: his entry No. 108; "w".

563 (110). Feb. 11, 1794 John G Blount enters 640 ac; border: his entry No. 109; "w".

564 (111). Feb. 11, 1794 John G Blount enters 640 ac in Hyde Co; border: his entry No. 110; "w".

565 (112). Feb. 11, 1794 John G Blount enters 640 ac in Hyde Co; border: his entry No. 111; "w".

566 (113). Feb. 11, 1794 John G Blount enters 640 ac in Hyde Co; border: his entry No. 112; "w".

567 (114). Feb. 11, 1794 John G Blount enters 640 ac in Hyde Co; border: his entry No. 113; "w".

568 (115). Feb. 11, 1794 John G Blount enters 640 ac in Hyde Co; border: his entry No. 114; "w".

569 (116). Feb. 11, 1794 John G Blount enters 640 ac in Hyde Co; border: his entry No. 115; "w".

page 28
570 (117). Feb. 11, 1794 John G Blount enters 640 ac; border: his entry No. 116; "w".

571 (118). Feb. 11, 1794 John G Blount enters 640 ac; border: his entry No. 117; "w".

572 (119). Feb. 11, 1794 John G Blount enters 640 ac; border: his entry No. 118; "w".

573 (120). Feb. 11, 1794 John G Blount enters 640 ac; border: his entry No. 119; "w".

574 (121). Feb. 11, 1794 John G Blount enters 640 ac; border: his entry No. 120; "w".

575 (122). Feb. 11, 1794 John G Blount enters 640 ac; border: his entry No. 121; "w".

576 (123). Feb. 11, 1794 John G Blount enters 640 ac; border: his entry No. 122; "w".

577 (124). Feb. 11, 1794 John G Blount enters 640 ac; border: his entry No. 123; "w".

page 29
578 (125). Feb. 11, 1794 John G Blount enters 640 ac; border: his entry No. 124; "w".

579 (126). Feb. 11, 1794 John G Blount enters 640 ac; border: his entry No. 125; "w".

580 (127). Feb. 11, 1794 John G Blount enters 640 ac; border: his entry No. 126; "w".

581 (128). Feb. 11, 1794 John G Blount enters 640 ac; border: his entry No. 127; "w".

582 (129). Feb. 11, 1794 John G Blount enters 640 ac in Hyde Co; border: his entry No. 128; "w".

583 (130). Feb. 11, 1794 John G Blount enters 640 ac in Hyde Co; border: his entry No. 129; "w".

584 (131). Feb. 11, 1794 John G Blount enters 640 ac in Hyde Co; border: his entry No. 130; "w".

585 (132). Feb. 11, 1794 John G Blount enters 640 ac in Hyde Co; border: his entry No. 131; "w".

page 30

586 (133). Feb. 11, 1794 John G Blount enters 640 ac in Hyde Co; border: his entry No. 132; warrant issued.

587 (134). Feb. 11, 1794 John G Blount enters 640 ac in Hyde Co; border: his entry No. 133; warrant issued.

588 (135). Feb. 11, 1794 John G Blount enters 640 ac in Hyde Co; border: his entry No. 134; warrant issued.

589 (136). Feb. 11, 1794 John G Blount enters 640 ac in Hyde Co; border: his entry No. 135; warrant issued.

590 (137). Feb. 11, 1794 John G Blount enters 640 ac in Hyde Co; border: his entry No. 136; warrant issued.

591 (138). Feb. 11, 1794 John G Blount enters 640 ac in Hyde Co; border: his entry No. 137; warrant issued.

592 (139). Feb. 11, 1794 John G Blount enters 640 ac in Hyde Co; border: his entry No. 138; warrant issued.

593 (140). Feb. 11, 1794 John G Blount enters 640 ac in Hyde Co; border: his entry No. 139; warrant issued.

page 31

594 (141). Feb. 11, 1794 John G Blount enters 640 ac on Mattamuskeet Lake, W side aof Wysoching Cr, & runs S and E; border: Henry Selby and Mulberry Ridge; warrant issued.

595 (142). Feb. 11, 1794 John G Blount enters 640 ac; border: his entry No. 141; warrant issued.

596 (143). Feb. 11, 1794 John G Blount enters 640 ac; border: his entry No. 142; warrant issued.

597 (144). Feb. 11, 1794 John G Blount enters 640 ac; border: his entry No. 143; warrant issued.

598 (145). Feb. 11, 1794 John G Blount enters 640 ac on W side of Wysoching Cr; border: Henry Selby on Mulberry Ridge and runs S & E; warrant issued.

599 (146). Feb. 11, 1794 John G Blount enters 640 ac in Hyde Co; border: his entry No. 145; warrant issued.

600 (147). Feb. 11, 1794 John G Blount enters 640 ac in Hyde Co; border: his entry No. 146; warrant issued.

601 (148). Feb. 11, 1794 John G Blount enters 640 ac in Hyde Co; border: his entry No. 147; warrant issued.

page 32
602 (149). Feb. 11, 1794 John G Blount enters 640 ac in Hyde Co; border: his entry No. 148; warrant issued.

603 (150). Feb. 11, 1794 John G Blount enters 640 ac in Hyde Co on Pungo Creek Swamp; border: back of M Windley; warrant issued.

604 (151). Feb. 11, 1794 John G Blount enters 640 ac in Hyde Co; border: his entry No. 150 and runs "towards" th head of Pungo R; warrant issued.
605 (152). Feb. 11, 1794 John G Blount enters 640 ac; border: his entry No. 151 and runs "towards" the head of Pungo R; warrant issued.

606 (153). Feb. 11, 1794 John G Blount enters 640 ac; border: his entry No. 152 and runs "towards" the head of Pungo R; warrant issued.

607 (154). Feb. 11, 1794 John G Blount enters 640 ac; border: his entry No. 153 and runs "towards" the head of Pungo R; warrant issued.

608 (155). Feb. 11, 1794 John G Blount enters 640 ac on the head of Long Shoal R; warrant issued.

609 (156). Feb. 11, 1794 John G Blount enters 640 ac on the head of Long Shoal R; border: his entry No. 155; warrant issued.

page 33
610 (157). Feb. 11, 1794 John G Blount enters 640 ac; border: his entry No. 156; warrant issued.

611 (158). Feb. 11, 1794 John G Blount enters 640 ac in Hyde Co; border: his entry No. 157; warrant issued.

612 (159). Feb. 11, 1794 John G Blount enters 640 ac; border: his entry No. 158.

613 (160). Feb. 11, 1794 John G Blount enters 640 ac; border: his entry No. 159; "w".

614 (161). Feb. 11, 1794 John G Blount enters 640 ac; border: his entry No. 160; "w".

615 (162). Feb. 11, 1794 John G Blount enters 640 ac in Hyde Co; border: his entry No. 161; "w".

616 (163). Feb. 11, 1794 John G Blount enters 640 ac; border: his entry No. 162; "w".

617 (164). Feb. 11, 1794 John G Blount enters 640 ac in Hyde Co; border: his entry No. 163; "w".

618 (165). Feb. 11, 1794 John G Blount enters 640 ac in Hyde Co; border: his entry No. 164.

page 34
619 (166). Feb. 11, 1794 John G Blount enters 640 ac; border: entry No. 165; warrant issued.

620 (167). Feb. 11, 1794 John G Blount enters 640 ac; border: entry No. 166; warrant issued.

621 (168). Feb. 11, 1794 John G Blount enters 640 ac in Hyde Co; border: entry No. 167; warrant issued.

622 (169). Feb. 11, 1794 John G Blount enters 640 ac in Hyde Co; border: entry No. 168; warrant issued.

623 (170). Feb. 11, 1794 John G Blount enters 640 ac in Hyde Co; border: entry No. 169; warrant issued.

624 (171). Feb. 23, 1794 Joseph Keach enters 100 ac on W side of Pungo R and the head of Turkey Br; border: Senhler Jordan, Ben Foreman, &James Baily; warrant issued.

625 (172). Feb. 24, 1794 William Carrowon enters 74 ac on E side of Swan Quarter Bay; border: John Smith's W corner, runs to a corner of his own patent,

& with his line to the beginning; being within the bounds of his own patent; warrant issued.

page 35

626 (173). Feb. 24, 1794 William Harris enters 500 ac; border: John Swindell's patent on N side of Mattamuskeet Lake, William Bomar's corner at the back line of said patent, & runs E and N; warrant issued "none".

627 (174). Mar. 8, 1794 Lovit Bell enters 50 ac on S side of Mattamuskeet Lake; border: Ellison's patent, George Tarner's patent, & William Watson; warrant issued.

628 (175). Apr. 8, 1794 William Clark enters 15 ac; between Brite's patent and Jones Cr; warrant issued.

629 (176). Apr. 22, 1794 John G Blount enters 640 ac in Hyde Co; border: the surveyed land on NE side of Mattamusket Lake and runs "towards" Long Shoal R; warrant issued.

630 (177). Apr. 22, 1794 John G Blount enters 640 ac in Hyde Co; border: his foregoing entries; warrant issued.

page 36

631 (178). Apr. 22, 1794 John G Blount enters 640 ac in Hyde Co; border: his foregoing entries; warrant issued.

632 (179). Apr. 22, 1794 John G Blount enters 640 ac in Hyde Co; border: his foregoing entries; warrant issued.

633 (180). Apr. 22, 1794 John G Blount enters 640 ac in Hyde Co; border: his foregoing entries; warrant issued.

634 (181). Apr. 22, 1794 John G Blount enters 640 ac in Hyde Co; border: his foregoing entries; warrant issued.

635 (182). Apr. 22, 1794 John G Blount enters 640 ac in Hyde Co; border: his foregoing entries; warrant issued.

636 (183). Apr. 22, 1794 John G Blount enters 640 ac in Hyde Co; border: his foregoing entries; warrant issued.

637 (184). Apr. 22, 1794 John G Blount enters 640 ac in Hyde Co; border: his foregoing entries; warrant issued.

638 (185). Apr. 22, 1794 John G Blount enters 640 ac in Hyde Co; border: his foregoing entries; warrant issued.

page 37

639 (186). Apr. 22, 1794 John G Blount enters 640 ac in Hyde Co; border: his foregoing entries; warrant issued.

640 (187). Apr. 22, 1794 John G Blount enters 640 ac in Hyde Co; border: his foregoing entries; warrant issued.

641 (188). Apr. 22, 1794 John G Blount enters 640 ac in Hyde Co; border: his foregoing entries; warrant issued.

642 (189). Apr. 22, 1794 John G Blount enters 640 ac in Hyde Co; border: his foregoing entries; warrant issued.

643 (190). Apr. 22, 1794 John G Blount enters 640 ac in Hyde Co; border: his foregoing entries; warrant issued; [this entry written in the book twice].

644 (191). Apr. 22, 1794 John G Blount enters 640 ac in Hyde Co; border: his foregoing entries; warrant issued.

645 (192). Apr. 22, 1794 John G Blount enters 640 ac in Hyde Co; border: his foregoing entries; warrant issued.

646 (193). Apr. 22, 1794 John G Blount enters 640 ac in Hyde Co; border: his foregoing entries; warrant issued.

page 38

647 (194). Apr. 22, 1794 John G Blount enters 640 ac in Hyde Co; border: his foregoing entries; warrant issued.

648 (195). Apr. 22, 1794 John G Blount enters 640 ac in Hyde Co; border: his foregoing entries; warrant issued.

649 (196). Apr. 22, 1794 John G Blount enters 640 ac in Hyde Co; border: his foregoing entries; warrant issued.

650 (197). Apr. 22, 1794 John G Blount enters 640 ac in Hyde Co; border: his foregoing entries; warrant issued.

651 (198). Apr. 22, 1794 John G Blount enters 640 ac in Hyde Co; border: his foregoing entries; warrant issued.

652 (199). Apr. 22, 1794 John G Blount enters 640 ac in Hyde Co; border: his foregoing entries; warrant issued.

653 (200). Apr. 22, 1794 John G Blount enters 640 ac in Hyde Co; border: his foregoing entries; warrant issued.

page 39

654 (201). Apr. 22, 1794 John G Blount enters 640 ac in Hyde Co; border: his foregoing entries; warrant issued.

655 (202). Apr. 22, 1794 John G Blount enters 640 ac in Hyde Co; border: his foregoing entries; warrant issued.

656 (203). Apr. 22, 1794 John G Blount enters 640 ac in Hyde Co; border: his foregoing entries; warrant issued.

657 (204). Apr. 22, 1794 John G Blount enters 640 ac; border: his foregoing entries; warrant issued.

658 (205). Apr. 22, 1794 John G Blount enters 640 ac; border: his foregoing entries; warrant issued.

659 (206). Apr. 22, 1794 John G Blount enters 640 ac; border: his foregoing entries; warrant issued.

660 (207). Apr. 22, 1794 John G Blount enters 640 ac; border: his foregoing entries; warrant issued.

page 40

661 (208). Apr. 22, 1794 John G Blount enters 640 ac in Hyde Co; border: his foregoing entries; warrant issued.

662 (209). Apr. 22, 1794 John G Blount enters 640 ac in Hyde Co; border: his foregoing entries; warrant issued.

663 (210). Apr. 22, 1794 John G Blount enters 640 ac in Hyde Co; border: his foregoing entries; warrant issued.

664 (211). Apr. 22, 1794 John G Blount enters 640 ac in Hyde Co; border: his foregoing entries; warrant issued.

665 (212). Apr. 22, 1794 John G Blount enters 640 ac in Hyde Co; border: his foregoing entries; warrant issued.

666 (213). Apr. 22, 1794 John G Blount enters 640 ac in Hyde Co; border: his foregoing entries; warrant issued.

667 (214). Apr. 22, 1794 John G Blount enters 640 ac in Hyde Co; border: his foregoing entries; warrant issued.

page 41

668 (215). Apr. 22, 1794 John G Blount enters 640 ac in Hyde Co; border: his foregoing entries; warrant issued.

669 (216). Apr. 22, 1794 John G Blount enters 640 ac in Hyde Co; border: his foregoing entries; warrant issued.

670 (217). Apr. 22, 1794 John G Blount enters 640 ac in Hyde Co; border: his foregoing entries; warrant issued.
671 (218). Apr. 22, 1794 John G Blount enters 640 ac in Hyde Co; border: his foregoing entries; warrant issued.

672 (219). Apr. 22, 1794 John G Blount enters 640 ac in Hyde Co; border: his foregoing entries; warrant issued.

673 (220). Apr. 22, 1794 John G Blount enters 640 ac in Hyde Co; border: his foregoing entries; warrant issued.

674 (221). Apr. 22, 1794 John G Blount enters 640 ac in Hyde Co; border: his foregoing entries; warrant issued.

675 (222). Apr. 22, 1794 John G Blount enters 640 ac in Hyde Co; border: his foregoing entries; warrant issued.

676 (223). Apr. 22, 1794 John G Blount enters 640 ac in Hyde Co; border: his foregoing entries; warrant issued.

page 42
677 (224). Apr. 22, 1794 John G Blount enters 640 ac in Hyde Co; border: his foregoing entries; warrant issued.

678 (225). Apr. 22, 1794 John G Blount enters 640 ac in Hyde Co; border: his foregoing entries; warrant issued.

679 (226). Apr. 22, 1794 John G Blount enters 640 ac in Hyde Co; border: his foregoing entries; warrant issued.

680 (227). Apr. 22, 1794 John G Blount enters 640 ac in Hyde Co; border: his foregoing entries; warrant issued.

681 (228). Apr. 22, 1794 John G Blount enters 640 ac in Hyde Co; border: his foregoing entries; warrant issued.

682 (229). Apr. 22, 1794 John G Blount enters 640 ac in Hyde Co; border: his foregoing entries; warrant issued.

683 (230). Apr. 22, 1794 John G Blount enters 640 ac in Hyde Co; border: his foregoing entries; warrant issued.

684 (231). Apr. 22, 1794 John G Blount enters 640 ac in Hyde Co; border: his foregoing entries; warrant issued.

page 43
685 (232). Apr. 22, 1794 John G Blount enters 640 ac in Hyde Co; border: his foregoing entries; warrant issued.

686 (233). Apr. 22, 1794 John G Blount enters 640 ac in Hyde Co; border: his foregoing entries; warrant issued.

687 (234). Apr. 22, 1794 John G Blount enters 640 ac in Hyde Co; border: his foregoing entries; warrant issued.

688 (235). Apr. 22, 1794 John G Blount enters 640 ac in Hyde Co; border: his "above" entries; warrant issued.

689 (236). Apr. 22, 1794 John G Blount enters 640 ac in Hyde Co; border: his foregoing entries; warrant issued.

690 (237). Apr. 22, 1794 John G Blount enters 640 ac in Hyde Co; border: his foregoing entries; warrant issued.

691 (238). Apr. 22, 1794 John G Blount enters 640 ac in Hyde Co; border: his foregoing entries; warrant issued.

692 (239). Apr. 22, 1794 John G Blount enters 640 ac in Hyde Co; border: his foregoing entries; warrant issued.

page 44
693 (240). Apr. 22, 1794 John G Blount enters 640 ac in Hyde Co; border: his foregoing entries; warrant issued.

694 (241). Apr. 22, 1794 John G Blount enters 640 ac in Hyde Co; border: his foregoing entries; warrant issued.
695 (242). Apr. 22, 1794 John G Blount enters 640 ac in Hyde Co; border: his foregoing entries; warrant issued.

696 (243). Apr. 22, 1794 John G Blount enters 640 ac in Hyde Co; border: his foregoing entries; warrant issued.

697 (244). Apr. 22, 1794 John G Blount enters 640 ac in Hyde Co; border: his foregoing entries; warrant issued.

698 (245). Apr. 22, 1794 John G Blount enters 640 ac in Hyde Co; border: his foregoing entries; warrant issued.

699 (246). Apr. 22, 1794 John G Blount enters 640 ac in Hyde Co; border: his foregoing entries; warrant issued.

page 45
700 (247). George Matthews, for William Smith of Baltimore, enters 640 ac in Hyde Co; border: a tract claimed by John Hunt, begins at William Harris' land on E side of Mattamuskeet Lake, & runs N and E.

701 (248). May 30, 1794 George Matthews, for William Smith of Baltimore, enters 640 ac; border: his entry No. 247 of this day.

702 (249). May 30, 1794 George Matthews, for William Smith of Baltimore, enters 640 ac; border: his entry No. 248 of this day.

703 (250). May 30, 1794 George Matthews, for William Smith of Baltimore, enters 640 ac; border: his foregoing entries made this day.

704 (251). May 30, 1794 George Matthews, for William Smith of Baltimore, enters 640 ac; border: his foregoing entries made this day.

page 46
705 (252). Jun. 1, 1794 John G Blount enters 640 ac in Hyde Co between Pamplico and Albemarle Sounds; border: his foregoing entries; warrant issued.

706 (253). Jun. 1, 1794 John G Blount enters 640 ac in Hyde Co between Pamplico and Albemarle Sounds; border: his foregoing entries; warrant issued.

707 (254). Jun. 1, 1794 John G Blount enters 640 ac in Hyde Co between Pamplico and Albemarle Sounds; border: his foregoing entries; warrant issued.

708 (255). Jun. 1, 1794 John G Blount enters 640 ac in Hyde Co between Pamplico and Albemarle Sounds; border: his foregoing entries; warrant issued.

709 (256). Jun. 1, 1794 John G Blount enters 640 ac in Hyde Co between Pamplico and Albemarle Sounds; border: his foregoing entries; warrant issued.

710 (257). Jun. 1, 1794 John G Blount enters 640 ac in Hyde Co between Pamplico and Albemarle Sounds; border: his foregoing entries; warrant issued.

page 47
711 (258). Jun. 1, 1794 John G Blount enters 640 ac in Hyde Co between Pamplico and Albemarle Sounds; border: his foregoing entries; warrant issued.

712 (259). Jun. 1, 1794 John G Blount enters 640 ac in Hyde Co between Pamplico and Albemarle Sounds; border: his foregoing entries; warrant issued.

713 (260). Jun. 1, 1794 John G Blount enters 640 ac in Hyde Co between Pamplico and Albemarle Sounds; border: his foregoing entries; warrant issued.

714 (261). Jun. 1, 1794 John G Blount enters 640 ac in Hyde Co between Pamplico and Albemarle Sounds; border: his foregoing entries; warrant issued.

715 (262). Jun. 1, 1794 John G Blount enters 640 ac in Hyde Co between Pamplico and Albemarle Sounds; border: his foregoing entries; warrant issued.

716 (263). Jun. 1, 1794 John G Blount enters 640 ac in Hyde Co between Pamplico and Albemarle Sounds; border: his foregoing entries; warrant issued.

717 (264). Jun. 1, 1794 John G Blount enters 640 ac in Hyde Co between Pamplico and Albemarle Sounds; border: his foregoing entries; warrant issued.

page 48
718 (265). Jun. 1, 1794 John G Blount enters 640 ac in Hyde Co between Pamplico and Albemarle Sounds; border: his foregoing entries; warrant issued.

719 (266). Jun. 1, 1794 John G Blount enters 640 ac in Hyde Co between Pamplico and Albemarle Sounds; border: his foregoing entries; warrant issued.

720 (267). Jun. 1, 1794 John G Blount enters 640 ac in Hyde Co between Pamplico and Albemarle Sounds; border: his foregoing entries; warrant issued.

721 (268). Jun. 1, 1794 John G Blount enters 640 ac in Hyde Co between Pamplico and Albemarle Sounds; border: his foregoing entries; warrant issued.

722 (269). Jun. 1, 1794 John G Blount enters 640 ac in Hyde Co between Pamplico and Albemarle Sounds; border: his foregoing entries; warrant issued.

723 (270). Jun. 1, 1794 John G Blount enters 640 ac in Hyde Co between Pamplico and Albemarle Sounds; border: his foregoing entries; warrant issued.

page 49
724 (271). Jun. 1, 1794 John G Blount enters 640 ac in Hyde Co between Pamplico and Albemarle Sounds; border: his foregoing entries; warrant issued.

725 (272). Jun. 1, 1794 John G Blount enters 640 ac in Hyde Co between Pamplico and Albemarle Sounds; border: his foregoing entries; warrant issued.

726 (273). Jun. 1, 1794 John G Blount enters 640 ac in Hyde Co between Pamplico and Albemarle Sounds; border: his foregoing entries; warrant issued.

727 (274). Jun. 1, 1794 John G Blount enters 640 ac in Hyde Co between Pamplico and Albemarle Sounds; border: his foregoing entries; warrant issued.

728 (275). Jun. 1, 1794 John G Blount enters 640 ac in Hyde Co between Pamplico and Albemarle Sounds; border: his foregoing entries; warrant issued.

729 (276). Jun. 1, 1794 John G Blount enters 640 ac in Hyde Co between Pamplico and Albemarle Sounds; border: his foregoing entries; warrant issued.

page 50
730 (277). Jun. 1, 1794 John G Blount enters 640 ac in Hyde Co between Pamplico and Albemarle Sounds; border: his foregoing entries; warrant issued.

731 (278). Jun. 1, 1794 John G Blount enters 640 ac in Hyde Co between Pamplico and Albemarle Sounds; border: his foregoing entries; warrant issued.

732 (279). Jun. 1, 1794 John G Blount enters 640 ac in Hyde Co between Pamplico and Albemarle Sounds; border: his foregoing entries; warrant issued.

733 (280). Jun. 1, 1794 John G Blount enters 640 ac in Hyde Co between Pamplico and Albemarle Sounds; border: his foregoing entries; warrant issued.

734 (281). Jun. 1, 1794 John G Blount enters 640 ac in Hyde Co between Pamplico and Albemarle Sounds; border: his foregoing entries; warrant issued.

735 (282). Jun. 1, 1794 John G Blount enters 640 ac in Hyde Co between Pamplico and Albemarle Sounds; border: his foregoing entries; warrant issued.

page 51
736 (283). Jun. 1, 1794 John G Blount enters 640 ac in Hyde Co between Pamplico and Albemarle Sounds; border: his foregoing entries; warrant issued.

737 (284). Jun. 1, 1794 John G Blount enters 640 ac in Hyde Co between Pamplico and Albemarle Sounds; border: his foregoing entries; warrant issued.

738 (285). Jun. 1, 1794 John G Blount enters 640 ac in Hyde Co between Pamplico and Albemarle Sounds; border: his foregoing entries; warrant issued.

739 (286). Jun. 1, 1794 John G Blount enters 640 ac in Hyde Co between Pamplico and Albemarle Sounds; border: his foregoing entries; warrant issued.

740 (287). Jun. 1, 1794 John G Blount enters 640 ac in Hyde Co between Pamplico and Albemarle Sounds; border: his foregoing entries; warrant issued.

741 (288). Jun. 1, 1794 John G Blount enters 640 ac in Hyde Co between Pamplico and Albemarle Sounds; border: his foregoing entries; warrant issued.

page 52
742 (289). Jun. 1, 1794 John G Blount enters 640 ac in Hyde Co; border: his foregoing entries; warrant issued.

743 (290). Jun. 1, 1794 John G Blount enters 640 ac in Hyde Co; border: his foregoing entries; warrant issued.

744 (291). Jun. 1, 1794 John G Blount enters 640 ac in Hyde Co; border: his foregoing entries; warrant issued.
745 (292). Jun. 1, 1794 John G Blount enters 640 ac in Hyde Co; border: his foregoing entries; warrant issued.

746 (293). Jun. 1, 1794 John G Blount enters 640 ac in Hyde Co; border: his foregoing entries; warrant issued.

747 (294). Jun. 1, 1794 John G Blount enters 640 ac in Hyde Co; border: his foregoing entries; warrant issued.

748 (295). Jun. 1, 1794 John G Blount enters 640 ac in Hyde Co; border: his foregoing entries; warrant issued.

page 53
749 (296). Jun. 1, 1794 John G Blount enters 640 ac in Hyde Co between Pamplico and Albemarle Sounds; border: his foregoing entries; warrant issued.

750 (297). Jun. 1, 1794 John G Blount enters 640 ac in Hyde Co between Pamplico and Albemarle Sounds; border: his foregoing entries; warrant issued.

751 (298). Jun. 1, 1794 John G Blount enters 640 ac in Hyde Co between Pamplico and Albemarle Sounds; border: his foregoing entries; warrant issued.

752 (299). Jun. 1, 1794 John G Blount enters 640 ac in Hyde Co between Pamplico and Albemarle Sounds; border: his foregoing entries; warrant issued.

753 (300). Jun. 1, 1794 John G Blount enters 640 ac in Hyde Co between Pamplico and Albemarle Sounds; border: his foregoing entries; warrant issued.

754 (301). Jun. 1, 1794 John G Blount enters 640 ac in Hyde Co between Pamplico and Albemarle Sounds; border: his foregoing entries; warrant issued.

755 (302). Jun. 1, 1794 John G Blount enters 640 ac in Hyde Co between Pamplico and Albemarle Sounds; border: his foregoing entries; warrant issued.

page 54

756 (303). Jun. 1, 1794 John G Blount enters 640 ac in Hyde Co; border: his foregoing entries; warrant issued.

757 (304). Jun. 1, 1794 John G Blount enters 640 ac in Hyde Co; border: his foregoing entries; warrant issued.

758 (305). Jun. 1, 1794 John G Blount enters 640 ac in Hyde Co; border: his foregoing entries; warrant issued.

759 (306). Jun. 1, 1794 John G Blount enters 640 ac in Hyde Co; border: his foregoing entries; warrant issued.

760 (307). Jun. 1, 1794 John G Blount enters 640 ac in Hyde Co; border: his foregoing entries; warrant issued.

761 (308). Jun. 1, 1794 John G Blount enters 640 ac in Hyde Co; border: his foregoing entries; warrant issued.

762 (309). Jun. 1, 1794 John G Blount enters 640 ac in Hyde Co; border: his foregoing entries; warrant issued.

763 (310). Jun. 1, 1794 John G Blount enters 640 ac in Hyde Co; border: his foregoing entries; warrant issued.

page 55

764 (311). Jun. 1, 1794 John G Blount enters 640 ac in Hyde Co; border: his foregoing entries; warrant issued.

765 (312). Jun. 1, 1794 John G Blount enters 640 ac in Hyde Co; border: his foregoing entries; warrant issued.

766 (313). Jun. 1, 1794 John G Blount enters 640 ac in Hyde Co; border: his foregoing entries; warrant issued.

767 (314). Jun. 1, 1794 John G Blount enters 640 ac in Hyde Co between Pamplico and Albemarle Sounds; border: his foregoing entries; warrant issued.

768 (315). Jun. 1, 1794 John G Blount enters 640 ac in Hyde Co between Pamplico and Albemarle Sounds; border: his foregoing entries; warrant issued.

769 (316). Jun. 1, 1794 John G Blount enters 640 ac in Hyde Co between Pamplico and Albemarle Sounds; border: his foregoing entries; warrant issued.

770 (317). Jun. 1, 1794 John G Blount enters 640 ac in Hyde Co between Pamplico and Albemarle Sounds; border: his foregoing entries; warrant issued.

page 56
771 (318). Jun. 1, 1794 John G Blount enters 640 ac in Hyde Co between Pamplico and Albemarle Sounds; border: his foregoing entries; warrant issued.

772 (319). Jun. 1, 1794 John G Blount enters 640 ac in Hyde Co between Pamplico and Albemarle Sounds; border: his foregoing entries; warrant issued.

773 (320). Jun. 1, 1794 John G Blount enters 640 ac in Hyde Co between Pamplico and Albemarle Sounds; border: his foregoing entries; warrant issued.

774 (321). Jun. 1, 1794 John G Blount enters 640 ac in Hyde Co between Pamplico and Albemarle Sounds; border: his foregoing entries; warrant issued.

775 (322). Jun. 1, 1794 John G Blount enters 640 ac in Hyde Co between Pamplico and Albemarle Sounds; border: his foregoing entries; warrant issued.

776 (323). Jun. 1, 1794 John G Blount enters 640 ac in Hyde Co between Pamplico and Albemarle Sounds; border: his foregoing entries; warrant issued.

777 (324). Jun. 1, 1794 John G Blount enters 640 ac in Hyde Co between Pamplico and Albemarle Sounds; border: his foregoing entries; warrant issued.

page 57
778 (325). Jun. 1, 1794 John G Blount enters 640 ac in Hyde Co between Pamplico and Albemarle Sounds; border: his foregoing entries; warrant issued.

779 (326). Jun. 1, 1794 John G Blount enters 640 ac in Hyde Co between Pamplico and Albemarle Sounds; border: his foregoing entries; warrant issued.

780 (327). Jun. 1, 1794 John G Blount enters 640 ac in Hyde Co between Pamplico and Albemarle Sounds; border: his foregoing entries; warrant issued.

781 (328). Jun. 1, 1794 John G Blount enters 640 ac in Hyde Co between Pamplico and Albemarle Sounds; border: his foregoing entries; warrant issued.
782 (329). Jun. 1, 1794 John G Blount enters 640 ac in Hyde Co between Pamplico and Albemarle Sounds; border: his foregoing entries; warrant issued.

783 (330). Jun. 1, 1794 John G Blount enters 640 ac in Hyde Co between Pamplico and Albemarle Sounds; border: his foregoing entries; warrant issued.

784 (331). Jun. 1, 1794 John G Blount enters 640 ac in Hyde Co between Pamplico and Albemarle Sounds; border: his foregoing entries; warrant issued.

page 58

785 (332). Jun. 1, 1794 John G Blount enters 640 ac in Hyde Co between Pamplico and Albemarle Sounds; border: his foregoing entries; warrant issued.

786 (333). Jun. 1, 1794 John G Blount enters 640 ac in Hyde Co between Pamplico and Albemarle Sounds; border: his foregoing entries; warrant issued.

787 (334). Jun. 1, 1794 John G Blount enters 640 ac in Hyde Co between Pamplico and Albemarle Sounds; border: his foregoing entries; warrant issued.

788 (335). Jun. 1, 1794 John G Blount enters 640 ac in Hyde Co between Pamplico and Albemarle Sounds; border: his foregoing entries; warrant issued.

789 (336). Jun. 1, 1794 John G Blount enters 640 ac in Hyde Co between Pamplico and Albemarle Sounds; border: his foregoing entries; warrant issued.

790 (337). Jun. 1, 1794 John G Blount enters 640 ac in Hyde Co between Pamplico and Albemarle Sounds; border: his foregoing entries; warrant issued.

page 59
791 (338). Jun. 1, 1794 John G Blount enters 640 ac in Hyde Co between Pamplico and Albemarle Sounds; border: his foregoing entries; warrant issued.

792 (339). Jun. 1, 1794 John G Blount enters 640 ac in Hyde Co between Pamplico and Albemarle Sounds; border: his foregoing entries; warrant issued.

793 (340). Jun. 1, 1794 John G Blount enters 640 ac in Hyde Co between Pamplico and Albemarle Sounds; border: his foregoing entries; warrant issued.

794 (341). Jun. 1, 1794 John G Blount enters 640 ac in Hyde Co between Pamplico and Albemarle Sounds; border: his foregoing entries; warrant issued.

795 (342). Jun. 1, 1794 John G Blount enters 640 ac in Hyde Co between Pamplico and Albemarle Sounds; border: his foregoing entries; warrant issued.

796 (343). Jun. 1, 1794 John G Blount enters 640 ac in Hyde Co between Pamplico and Albemarle Sounds; border: his foregoing entries; warrant issued.

797 (344). Jun. 1, 1794 John G Blount enters 640 ac in Hyde Co between Pamplico and Albemarle Sounds; border: his foregoing entries; warrant issued.

page 60
798 (345). Jun. 1, 1794 John G Blount enters 640 ac in Hyde Co between Pamplico and Albemarle Sounds; border: his foregoing entries; warrant issued.

799 (346). Jun. 1, 1794 John G Blount enters 640 ac in Hyde Co between Pamplico and Albemarle Sounds; border: his foregoing entries; warrant issued.

800 (347). Jun. 1, 1794 John G Blount enters 640 ac in Hyde Co between Pamplico and Albemarle Sounds; border: his foregoing entries; warrant issued.

801 (348). Jun. 1, 1794 John G Blount enters 640 ac in Hyde Co between Pamplico and Albemarle Sounds; border: his foregoing entries; warrant issued.

802 (349). Jun. 1, 1794 John G Blount enters 640 ac in Hyde Co between Pamplico and Albemarle Sounds; border: his foregoing entries; warrant issued.

803 (350). Jun. 1, 1794 John G Blount enters 640 ac in Hyde Co between Pamplico and Albemarle Sounds; border: his foregoing entries; warrant issued.

804 (351). Jun. 1, 1794 John G Blount enters 640 ac in Hyde Co between Pamplico and Albemarle Sounds; border: his foregoing entries; warrant issued.

page 61
805 (352). Jun. 1, 1794 John G Blount enters 640 ac in Hyde Co between Pamplico and Albemarle Sounds; border: his foregoing entries; warrant issued.

806 (353). Jun. 1, 1794 John G Blount enters 640 ac in Hyde Co; border: his foregoing entries; warrant issued.

807 (354). Jun. 1, 1794 John G Blount enters 640 ac in Hyde Co; border: his foregoing entries; warrant issued.

808 (355). Jun. 1, 1794 John G Blount enters 640 ac in Hyde Co; border: his foregoing entries; warrant issued.

809 (356). Jun. 1, 1794 John G Blount enters 640 ac in Hyde Co; border: his foregoing entries; warrant issued.

810 (357). Jun. 1, 1794 John G Blount enters 640 ac in Hyde Co; border: his foregoing entries; warrant issued.

811 (358). Jun. 1, 1794 John G Blount enters 640 ac in Hyde Co; border: his foregoing entries; warrant issued.

page 62
812 (359). Jun. 1, 1794 John G Blount enters 640 ac in Hyde Co between Pamplico and Albemarle Sounds; border: his foregoing entries; warrant issued.

813 (360). Jun. 1, 1794 John G Blount enters 640 ac in Hyde Co between Pamplico and Albemarle Sounds; border: his foregoing entries; warrant issued.

814 (861). Jun. 1, 1794 John G Blount enters 640 ac in Hyde Co between Pamplico and Albemarle Sounds; border: his foregoing entries; warrant issued.

815 (362). Jun. 1, 1794 John G Blount enters 640 ac in Hyde Co between Pamplico and Albemarle Sounds; border: his foregoing entries; warrant issued.
816 (363). Jun. 1, 1794 John G Blount enters 640 ac in Hyde Co between Pamplico and Albemarle Sounds; border: his foregoing entries; warrant issued.

817 (364). Jun. 1, 1794 John G Blount enters 640 ac in Hyde Co between Pamplico and Albemarle Sounds; border: his foregoing entries; warrant issued.

page 63
818 (365). Jun. 1, 1794 John G Blount enters 640 ac in Hyde Co; border: his foregoing entries; warrant issued.

819 (366). Jun. 1, 1794 John G Blount enters 640 ac in Hyde Co; border: his foregoing entries; warrant issued.

820 (367). Jun. 1, 1794 John G Blount enters 640 ac in Hyde Co; border: his foregoing entries; warrant issued.

821 (368). Jun. 1, 1794 John G Blount enters 640 ac in Hyde Co; border: his foregoing entries; warrant issued.

822 (369). Jun. 1, 1794 John G Blount enters 640 ac in Hyde Co; border: his foregoing entries; warrant issued.

823 (370). Jun. 1, 1794 John G Blount enters 640 ac in Hyde Co; border: his foregoing entries; warrant issued.

824 (371). Jun. 1, 1794 John G Blount enters 640 ac in Hyde Co; border: his foregoing entries; warrant issued.

page 64
825 (372). Jun. 1, 1794 John G Blount enters 640 ac in Hyde Co; border: his foregoing entries; warrant issued.

826 (373). Jun. 1, 1794 John G Blount enters 640 ac in Hyde Co; border: his foregoing entries; warrant issued.

827 (374). Jun. 1, 1794 John G Blount enters 640 ac in Hyde Co; border: his foregoing entries; warrant issued.

828 (375). Jun. 1, 1794 John G Blount enters 640 ac in Hyde Co; border: his foregoing entries; warrant issued.

829 (376). Jun. 1, 1794 John G Blount enters 640 ac in Hyde Co; border: his foregoing entries; warrant issued.

830 (377). Jun. 1, 1794 John G Blount enters 640 ac in Hyde Co; border: his foregoing entries; warrant issued.

831 (378). Jun. 1, 1794 John G Blount enters 640 ac in Hyde Co; border: his foregoing entries; warrant issued.

page 65
832 (379). Jun. 1, 1794 John G Blount enters 640 ac in Hyde Co; border: his foregoing entries; warrant issued.

833 (380). Jun. 1, 1794 John G Blount enters 640 ac in Hyde Co; border: his foregoing entries; warrant issued.

834 (381). Jun. 1, 1794 John G Blount enters 640 ac in Hyde Co; border: his foregoing entries; warrant issued.

835 (382). Jun. 1, 1794 John G Blount enters 640 ac in Hyde Co; border: his foregoing entries; warrant issued.

836 (383). Jun. 1, 1794 John G Blount enters 640 ac in Hyde Co; border: his foregoing entries; warrant issued.

837 (384). Jun. 1, 1794 John G Blount enters 640 ac in Hyde Co; border: his foregoing entries; warrant issued.

838 (385). Jun. 1, 1794 John G Blount enters 640 ac in Hyde Co; border: his foregoing entries; warrant issued.
839 (386). Jun. 1, 1794 John G Blount enters 640 ac in Hyde Co; border: his foregoing entries; warrant issued.

page 66
840 (387). Jun. 1, 1794 John G Blount enters 640 ac in Hyde Co; border: his foregoing entries; warrant issued.

841 (388). Jun. 1, 1794 John G Blount enters 640 ac in Hyde Co; border: his foregoing entries; warrant issued.

842 (389). Jun. 1, 1794 John G Blount enters 640 ac in Hyde Co; border: his foregoing entries; warrant issued.

843 (390) Jun. 1, 1794 John G Blount enters 640 ac in Hyde Co; border: his foregoing entries; warrant issued.

844 (391). Jun. 1, 1794 John G Blount enters 640 ac in Hyde Co; border: his foregoing entries; warrant issued.

845 (392). Jun. 1, 1794 John G Blount enters 640 ac in Hyde Co; border: his foregoing entries; warrant issued.

846 (393). Jun. 1, 1794 John G Blount enters 640 ac in Hyde Co; border: his foregoing entries; warrant issued.

847 (394). Jun. 1, 1794 John G Blount enters 640 ac in Hyde Co; border: his foregoing entries; warrant issued.

page 67
848 (395). Jun. 1, 1794 John G Blount enters 640 ac in Hyde Co; border: his foregoing entries; warrant issued.

849 (396). Jun. 1, 1794 John G Blount enters 640 ac in Hyde Co between Pamplico and Albemarle Sounds; border: his foregoing entries; warrant issued.

850 (397). Jun. 1, 1794 John G Blount enters 640 ac in Hyde Co between Pamplico and Albemarle Sounds; border: his foregoing entries; warrant issued.

851 (398). Jun. 1, 1794 John G Blount enters 640 ac in Hyde Co between Pamplico and Albemarle Sounds; border: his foregoing entries; warrant issued.

852 (399). Jun. 1, 1794 John G Blount enters 640 ac in Hyde Co between Pamplico and Albemarle Sounds; border: his foregoing entries; warrant issued.

853 (400). Jun. 1, 1794 John G Blount enters 640 ac in Hyde Co; border: his foregoing entries; warrant issued.

854 (401). Jun. 1, 1794 John G Blount enters 640 ac in Hyde Co; border: his foregoing entries; warrant issued.

page 68
855 (402). Jun. 1, 1794 John G Blount enters 640 ac in Hyde Co; border: his foregoing entries; warrant issued.

856 (403). Jun. 1, 1794 John G Blount enters 640 ac in Hyde Co; border: his foregoing entries; warrant issued.

857 (404). Jun. 1, 1794 John G Blount enters 640 ac in Hyde Co; border: his foregoing entries; warrant issued.

858 (405). Jun. 1, 1794 John G Blount enters 640 ac in Hyde Co; border: his foregoing entries; warrant issued.

859 (406). Jun. 1, 1794 John G Blount enters 640 ac in Hyde Co between Pamplico and Albemarle Sounds; border: his foregoing entries; warrant issued.

860 (407). Jun. 1, 1794 John G Blount enters 640 ac in Hyde Co between Pamplico and Albemarle Sounds; border: his foregoing entries; warrant issued.

861 (408). Jun. 1, 1794 John G Blount enters 640 ac in Hyde Co between Pamplico and Albemarle Sounds; border: his foregoing entries; warrant issued.

page 69
862 (409). Jun. 1, 1794 John G Blount enters 640 ac in Hyde Co between Pamplico and Albemarle Sounds; border: his foregoing entries; warrant issued.

863 (410). Jun. 1, 1794 John G Blount enters 640 ac in Hyde Co between Pamplico and Albemarle Sounds; border: his foregoing entries; warrant issued.

864 (411). Jun. 1, 1794 John G Blount enters 640 ac in Hyde Co between Pamplico and Albemarle Sounds; border: his foregoing entries; warrant issued.

865 (412). Jun. 1, 1794 John G Blount enters 640 ac in Hyde Co between Pamplico and Albemarle Sounds; border: his foregoing entries; warrant issued.

866 (413). Jun. 1, 1794 John G Blount enters 640 ac in Hyde Co between Pamplico and Albemarle Sounds; border: his foregoing entries; warrant issued.

867 (414). Jun. 1, 1794 John G Blount enters 640 ac in Hyde Co between Pamplico and Albemarle Sounds; border: his foregoing entries; warrant issued.

868 (415). Jun. 1, 1794 John G Blount enters 640 ac in Hyde Co between Pamplico and Albemarle Sounds; border: his foregoing entries; warrant issued.

869 (416). Jun. 1, 1794 John G Blount enters 640 ac in Hyde Co between Pamplico and Albemarle Sounds; border: his foregoing entries; warrant issued.

page 70
870 (417). Jun. 1, 1794 John G Blount enters 640 ac in Hyde Co; border: his foregoing entries; warrant issued.

871 (418). Jun. 1, 1794 John G Blount enters 640 ac in Hyde Co between Pamplico and Albemarle Sounds; border: his foregoing entries; warrant issued.

872 (419). Jun. 1, 1794 John G Blount enters 640 ac in Hyde Co between Pamplico and Albemarle Sounds; border: his foregoing entries; warrant issued.

873 (420). Jun. 1, 1794 John G Blount enters 640 ac in Hyde Co between Pamplico and Albemarle Sounds; border: his foregoing entries; warrant issued.

874 (421). Jun. 1, 1794 John G Blount enters 640 ac in Hyde Co; border: his foregoing entries; warrant issued.

875 (422). Jun. 1, 1794 John G Blount enters 640 ac in Hyde Co between Pamplico and Albemarle Sounds; border: his foregoing entries; warrant issued.

876 (423). Jun. 1, 1794 John G Blount enters 640 ac in Hyde Co between Pamplico and Albemarle Sounds; border: his foregoing entries; warrant issued.
877 (424). Jun. 1, 1794 John G Blount enters 640 ac in Hyde Co between Pamplico and Albemarle Sounds; border: his foregoing entries; warrant issued.

page 71
878 (425). Jun. 1, 1794 John G Blount enters 640 ac in Hyde Co between Pamplico and Albemarle Sounds; border: his foregoing entries; warrant issued.

879 (426). Jun. 1, 1794 John G Blount enters 640 ac in Hyde Co between Pamplico and Albemarle Sounds; border: his foregoing entries; warrant issued.

880 (427). Jun. 1, 1794 John G Blount enters 640 ac in Hyde Co; border: his foregoing entries; warrant issued.

881 (428). Jun. 1, 1794 John G Blount enters 640 ac in Hyde Co; border: his foregoing entries; warrant issued.

882 (429). Jun. 1, 1794 John G Blount enters 640 ac in Hyde Co; border: his foregoing entries; warrant issued.

883 (430). Jun. 1, 1794 John G Blount enters 640 ac in Hyde Co; border: his foregoing entries; warrant issued.

884 (431). Jun. 1, 1794 John G Blount enters 640 ac in Hyde Co; border: his foregoing entries; warrant issued.

885 (432). Jun. 1, 1794 John G Blount enters 640 ac in Hyde Co; border: his foregoing entries; warrant issued.

page 72
886 (433). Jun. 1, 1794 John G Blount enters 640 ac in Hyde Co between Pamplico and Albemarle Sounds; border: his foregoing entries; warrant issued.

887 (434). Jun. 1, 1794 John G Blount enters 640 ac in Hyde Co between Pamplico and Albemarle Sounds; border: his foregoing entries; warrant issued.

888 (435). Jun. 1, 1794 John G Blount enters 640 ac in Hyde Co between Pamplico and Albemarle Sounds; border: his foregoing entries; warrant issued.

889 (436). Jun. 1, 1794 John G Blount enters 640 ac in Hyde Co between Pamplico and Albemarle Sounds; border: his foregoing entries; warrant issued.

890 (437). Jun. 1, 1794 John G Blount enters 640 ac in Hyde Co between Pamplico and Albemarle Sounds; border: his foregoing entries; warrant issued.

891 (438). Jun. 1, 1794 John G Blount enters 640 ac in Hyde Co between Pamplico and Albemarle Sounds; border: his foregoing entries; warrant issued.

892 (439). Jun. 1, 1794 John G Blount enters 640 ac in Hyde Co between Pamplico and Albemarle Sounds; border: his foregoing entries; warrant issued.

page 73
893 (440). Jun. 1, 1794 John G Blount enters 640 ac in Hyde Co between Pamplico and Albemarle Sounds; border: his foregoing entries; warrant issued.

894 (441). Jun. 1, 1794 John G Blount enters 640 ac in Hyde Co between Pamplico and Albemarle Sounds; border: his foregoing entries; warrant issued.
895 (442). Jun. 1, 1794 John G Blount enters 640 ac in Hyde Co between Pamplico and Albemarle Sounds; border: his foregoing entries; warrant issued.

896 (443). Jun. 1, 1794 John G Blount enters 640 ac in Hyde Co between Pamplico and Albemarle Sounds; border: his foregoing entries; warrant issued.

897 (444). Jun. 1, 1794 John G Blount enters 640 ac in Hyde Co between Pamplico and Albemarle Sounds; border: his foregoing entries; warrant issued.

898 (445). Jun. 1, 1794 John G Blount enters 640 ac in Hyde Co between Pamplico and Albemarle Sounds; border: his foregoing entries; warrant issued.

899 (446). Jun. 1, 1794 John G Blount enters 640 ac in Hyde Co between Pamplico and Albemarle Sounds; border: his foregoing entries; warrant issued.

page 74
900 (447). Jun. 1, 1794 John G Blount enters 640 ac in Hyde Co between Pamplico and Albemarle Sounds; border: his foregoing entries; warrant issued.

901 (448). Jun. 1, 1794 John G Blount enters 640 ac in Hyde Co between Pamplico and Albemarle Sounds; border: his foregoing entries; warrant issued.

902 (449). Jun. 1, 1794 John G Blount enters 640 ac in Hyde Co between Pamplico and Albemarle Sounds; border: his foregoing entries; warrant issued.

903 (450). Jun. 1, 1794 John G Blount enters 640 ac in Hyde Co between Pamplico and Albemarle Sounds; border: his foregoing entries; warrant issued.

904 (451). Jun. 1, 1794 John G Blount enters 640 ac in Hyde Co between Pamplico and Albemarle Sounds; border: his foregoing entries; warrant issued.

904A [no number]. Jun. 1, 1794 John G Blount enters 640 ac in Hyde Co between Pamplico and Albemarle Sounds; border: his foregoing entries; warrant issued.

"End of J G Blount Entries"

page 75
905 (452). Jun. 27, 1794 Benjamin Russel enters 150 ac; border: his own line and William Russel's line near the Great Ridge.

906 (453). Jun. 30, 1794 Benjamin Foreman enters 100 ac; border: his own line on N side of Pungo Cr; warrant issued.

907 (454). Jun. 30, 1794 Benjamin Foreman enters 100 [60--lined out] ac; border: Colonel John Eborn's line, Jordan's line, Horth, Martin, & Eborn; warrant issued.

908 (455). Jul. 30, 1794 John Aldorson enters 1 ac in the mouth of Slade Cr and on E side of Pungo R; border: N corner of his Quay or pier, runs WSW "half" S 13 poles, SSE "half" E 13 poles, ENE "half" N 13 poles, NNW "half" W 13 poles to the beginning.

909 (456). Sept. 1, 1794 Richard Harvey enters 150 ac on W side of Pungo R; border: above Pine Grove Ridge and runs to said Harvey's new entry.

page 76   [blank page]
[on back cover]   "Entry book starts in 1790 and ended in 1794" [signed] Lathram.

next "book" has four loose sheets bound together or pages 1-8:
page 1
910 (1). Nov. 25, 1794 [top of page torn] in Hyde Co on S side of Mattamuskeet Lake; border: Peter Carter's patent, back of Weston's patent, said Carter's North [or NE--faint] corner, & runs W; issued.

911 (2). Nov. 25, 1794 Wm Watson sr enters 60 ac in Hyde Co on S side of Mattamuskeet Lake; border: said Wm Watson's "olde" Patent, Israel Watson, & said William Watson's new survey; issued.

912 (3). Nov. 26, 1794 Wm Harris enters 150 ac in Hyde Co on the head of Matamuskeet Lake; border: Robert Pormer's patent and runs with the lake to Jones' patent; issued.

913 (4). Nov. 26,1794 Zachariah Jarvis enters 65 ac in Hyde Co on Swan Quarter [Bay]; part of the surplus land in Roger Mason's patent; border: Thomas Mason's back corner, runs down Oystere Cr, to "the" head, & joins the "direct course" of Francis Credle's plat; entered before me W. Russel, JP; issued.

914 (5). Nov. 26, 1794 W Russel enters 50 ac in Hyde Co; within the bounds of Jonathan Jasper's patent at the head of Broad Cr and on E side of Pungo R; issued.

page 2
915 (6). Nov. 26, 1794 [top of page torn] enters 150 ac in Hyde Co on S side of Mattamuskeet Lake; border: Weston's line, Blount's survey, & William Carrawon's line; issued.

916 (7). Nov. 28, 1794 John Benjon enters 100 ac in Hyde Co on S side of Matamuskeet Lake; border: Wm Watson; issued.

917 (8). Dec. 15, 1794 Christopher Swindell enters 300 ac in Hyde Co on W side of Hern Bay; [being] the surplus land in James Clayton's patent; border: runs with said bay "on" Mattamuskeet Lake; issued.

918 (9). Dec. 15, 1794 Foster Jarvis sr enters 100 ac in Hyde Co on Swan Quarter [Bay]; border: Foster Jarvis' back corner, runs with said Jarvis' line, Josiah Jarvis' line of his "olde" patent, & said Josiah Jarvis' new patent lines; issued.

919 (10). Dec. 20, 1794 Anthony Tuley, son of Thomas Tuley, enters 150 ac on Swan Quarter [Bay]; being the surplus land in Josiah Jarvis' oldest patent on E side of Swan Quarter Bay; between Thomas Tuley's "plantation" and the middle of a drean between John Coffy's "plantation" & the division formerly made between Josiah Jarvis & Thomas Tuley "from the back line down to the water"; issued.

page 3
920 (11). Dec. 20 [written over 19], 1794 [Josiah ?--page torn] Jarvis enters [page torn] five ac in Hyde Co on Swan Quarter [Bay]; being surplus land in Cleeves' patent; border: Foster Jarvis' back corner, runs N22E to the patent line, & to Benjamin Mason's line, & to the beginning; issued.

921 (12). Dec. 20 [written over 19], 1794 James Jarvis enters 75 ac in Hyde Co on Swan Quarter [Bay] and the head of middle prong of Ouster Cr; border:

Zachariah Jarvis' line, Josiah Jarvis' entry, Foster Jarvis' patent, & runs to the head of Olde house Cr; issued.

922 (13). Dec. 20, 1794 Francis Credle enters 250 ac in Hyde Co on Swan Quarter [Bay]; being the surplus land in said Credle's patent; border: Smith, Hutson, & Mason; issued.

923 (14). Dec. 20, 17994 Samuel Weston enters 100 ac in Hyde Co on S side of Mattamuskeet Lake and SW side of Hern Bay; border: Christopher Swindell's entry, runs with the bay "up", & across "the" ridge, & "various courses" to Swindell's entry; issued.

924 (15). Dec. 20, 1794 William Carrawon enters 25 ac in Hyde Co on S side of Mattamuskeet Lake; border: the "corner bounder" between David Green and Wm Carrawon "in" Juniper Bay Road, in the back line of "our" front land, on David Green's line, John Eborn's line, my new patent, & with the back line of my front land to the beginning; issued.

page 4
925 (16). Jan. 1, 1795 Benjamin Gibbs enters [page torn] ac in Hyde Co on Mattamuskeet Lake; border: Clayton's line where Leech's line strikes it, with Clayton's line to Gibbs' "long" patent, with Gibbs' line to Swindell's line, with Swindell's line to Wm Cohoon, with Cohoon's line to Leech's line, & with Leech's line to the beginning; issued.

926 (17). Jan. 1, 1795 Nicholas Brin enters 200 ac in Hyde Co on N side of Mattamuskeet Lake; border: Jordan, runs with Swindell's line to Parmer's line, & with "Prmer's" line; issued.

927 (18). Mar. 3, 1795 James Eborn enters 100 ac in Hyde Co on N side of Pungo R; border: James Eborn's entry and on said Eborn's line; warrant.

928 (19). May 25, 1795 Benjamin Russel enters 100 ac in Hyde Co on E side of Pungo R in Currituck; border: my own land, Sauthey Rew, Anthony Tuley's patent, & my own corner tree in said Tuley's line; issued Oct. 19.

929 (20). May 25, 1795 Benjamin Russel enters 200 ac on W side of Pungo R; border: Wm Hodges Slade's entry, James Willikison's "supposed claim", & Dips Cr; issued.

page 5
930 (21). Jun. 8, 1794 [page torn]uel [page torn] in Hyde Co in New Currituck; border: John Proctor's NW corner, runs with Thomas Mason's line down the creek, & joins Tuley and Proctor; issued.

931 (22). Jun. 13, 1795 John Allen enters 640 ac in Hyde Co on W side of Pungo R and E side of Pungo Cr; border: J P Stakesbouy, Eborn, & Hollowell; known as the ready ground.

932 (23). Jun. 13, 1795 John Gibbs enters 50 ac in Hyde Co on E side of Long Shole R; known as "the" sand hills; border: Pains Bay and the sound to Eborn's line.

933 (24). Jul. 14, 1795 John Alderson enters 250 ac on E side of Pungo R and S side of Slades Cr; between the land held by Archabel McCorty, Simon Alderson, John Alderson "aforesaid", & James Hernton "in right of his wife"; issued.

page 6
934 (25). Aug. 21, 1795 John [page torn]field enters [page torn] ac on E side of Uper Dowry Cr; border: "olde" Richard Winfield's line.
935 (26). Oct. 2, 1795 Samuel Mason enters 50 ac in Hyde Co in New "Curituck"; border: Wm Ester's beginning near "the" branch of Deep Cr, "his" line, Thomas Mason, & Proctor; issued.

936 (27). Oct. 2, 1795 David Green, John Sadler, Samuel "Seby", & Nathan "Sebby" enter 640 ac in Hyde Co on Swan Quarter [Bay]; border: John Sadler and Joseph Picquit.

937 (28). Oct. 2, 1795 David Green, John Sadler, Samuel Selby, & Nathan Selby enters 640 ac in Hyde Co on Swan Quarter [Bay]; border: said Green's, Sadler's, & Selby's first entry.

938 (29). Oct. 15, 1795 Josiah Jarvis enters 500 ac in Hyde Co on Swan Quarter [Bay]; border: the head of Well Cr "or" Juniper Bay, runs with my new patent, May Caffy's deed, & "the" waters.

page 7
939 (30). Oct. 15, 1795 [page torn] 25 ac in Hyde Co on Swan Quarter [Bay]; being the surplus land in the bounds of my great patent; border: at [head--lined out] Well Point at Juniper Bay and runs with my line "towards" [Juniper Bay--lined out] "the" post oak ridge.

940 (31). Oct. 15, 1795 John Caffy enters 125 ac in Hyde Co on Swan Quarter [Bay]; border: Anthony tuley's entry, Josiah Jarvis' old patent, "the" water, & Josiah Jarvis' new patent.

941 (32). Oct. 16, 1795 Francis Credle enters 350 ac in Hyde Co on Swan Quarter [Bay]; border: Smith's patent, John Faddrey's patent, & McCarty's patent.

# Hyde County, NC Land Entries 1778-1795

942 (33). Oct. 16, 1795 David Jarvis enters 600 ac in Hyde Co on Swan Quarter [Bay]; border: Handcock's patent, Bloint's [or Ploint] patent, & Southay Rew's patent.

"Containing all the entries entered in my office"   [signed] Z Jarvis, E T

page 8   "D Green's Entry"

# Index to Hyde County, NC Land Entries


Abrams,   159
Abrams (Abram), John   144,
  168, 421, 526
Acollowell, Joseph jr   133
Addams (Adams), Thomas   71,
  331, 333
Albert, William   244
Albert, William sr   493
Alderson,   245
Alderson (Aldorson, Aldrson),
  John   340, 341, 358, 359,
  369, 507, 908, 933
Alderson, Jon   336
Alderson, Simon (Simond)
  360, 370, 389, 933
Aldorson, Thomas   535
Allen (Allin), Jesse   130, 131,
  230, 415, 438
Allen, John   130, 131, 372,
  375, 379-386, 408, 418, 424,
  931
Allen, Nathaniel   322
Anderson, Leah   70
Antry,   319
Armstrong, Gen.   482
Arnal (Arnol),   71
Arthur, John   270
Bachlor, James   450
Bailey, David   168
Bailey, Jesse   12, 168
Baily,   379
Baily, Bethuell   404
Baily, James   138, 624
Baily, Jesse N   138, 425, 433,
  434
Baily (Baley), Simon   347,
  352, 400
Baily (Bailey), Thomas   12,
  399
Ballance, Richard   247, 436
Bamey, Benjamin   464
Banks,   245
Banks, Abraham (Abam,
  Abram)   104, 125, 126, 137,
  179
Banks, Ann   87, 387, 412

Banks, Robert   387
Banks, William   412, 370
Barnes, Benjamin   361
Barnet,   279
Barnet, Robert   361
Barnet, Benjn   257
Barret, Bejamin   255
Barret, Robert   268
Barrow,   424
Barrow, George   53, 213, 225,
  283, 441
Barrow, George jr   213
Barrow, Thomas   69
Barrow, Zachariah (Zaceriah)
  213, 283, 422, 441
Bartee,   Reuben   (Ruben,   Rubin)
90, 91, 150, 151, 369, 371,
  376
Barter, Reuben   277
Bedford, Thomas   33
Bell, Dickson   117
Bell, Lovit   627
Bell, Morris   368
Bell, William   117
Bemey, Benjamin   465
Benjon, John   916
Benson, John   493, 494, 538
Benson, Reuben   538
Bishop (Boshop, Bushop),
  William   34, 57, 337
Blackledge, Richard   172, 196,
  215-223, 254, 286-305
Blackledge, Thomas   379
Blount (Bloint),   915, 942
Blount (Blunt), John G   312,
  545-623, 629-699, 705-904A
Blunt, Fedrick   258
Boey,   459
Bomar, William   626
Booty,   245, 247
Booty, Richard   436
Booty, William   524
Bray, James   343
Bray, John   466, 474
Bray, John sr   478, 518
Bright (Brite),   263, 278,

443, 628
Bright, John   122, 122
Bright, Simon   427
Brin, Nicholas   926
Brooke, Stephen   95
Bryan, John   364, 367
Burges,   200
Burgess, Malica (Malika)   212, 277
Caffy, John   940
Caffy, May   938
Cambell,   377
Campbel, William   85
Campbell, Vineard   281
Campbell, William   37, 88
Capps, Mathew (Mathaw)   72, 176
Capps, Richard   12, 107, 132, 159
Caps, John   210
Carrowon (Carronon, Carrawan, Carrowin), William   100, 155, 473, 480, 625, 915, 924
Carter, George   56
Carter, Peter   188, 910
Chambers,   144
Chambers, Caleb   11
Chambers, John   11, 526
Chambers, John sr   504
Chapman, Samuel   148
Chapple,   80
Cipps, Seth   425, 452
Clark, Henry   491
Clark, James   44, 55
Clark, Major   266, 267, 314, 327
Clark, Thomas   44, 506
Clark, William   347, 534, 543, 628
Clayton (Claton),   467, 509, 515, 925
Clayton, Elliott   457, 475, 505
Clayton, James   95, 457, 514, 533, 917
Clayton, William   533

Cleaves, Benjamin   415
Cleeves,   920
Cleeves (Cleves), James   180, 183-185, 239, 250, 275, 306, 312
Clipps, Seth   405
Coffy, John   919
Cohoon, William   479, 495, 925
Collins, Josiah   322
Collins, and Company   545
Cooprs, John   467
Cording,   143
Cording, Benjamin   62
Cording, Joseph   486
Cording, Thomas   486
Cording, William   392
Corrowone,   309
Coston,   158
Cove, Timothy   224
Coves, Molley T   285
Cox,   144, 504
Cox, Aaron (Aron)   129, 271
Cradell, Francis   249
Credle (Cradell, Crudle, Crudler), Francis   459, 468, 510, 913, 922, 941
Curtis, Joseph   431
Cutrel,   224
Daccson, James   516
Daily, William   502
Danels, Daniel   232
Darden, Jacob   544
Davenport (Devenport), George   22, 39, 193
Davenport, Joel   193, 194
Davis,   31
Davis, David   105, 155
Davis, James   336
Davis, Jesse   530
Davis (Daves), John   205, 207, 245, 284, 341, 412, 431
Davis, John jr   531, 532
Davis, John sr   536
Davis (Daves), Samuel   130, 264, 265, 331, 439, 446

# Index to Hyde County, NC Land Entries


Davis (Daves), William   28, 31, 50, 51, 59, 74, 189, 190, 245, 276, 524
Davison, James   49
Daw, William   444
Daws, Nicholas (Nicholes)   170, 197
Denison, George   39, 148
Dickeson, Samuel   322
Dike,   327
Dowery,   278
Duke, George   28, 29, 73, 176
Dukes, George sr   320
Dunbar, James   501
Durden (Durdin), David   257, 279
Durden, Elisha   257, 284
Durden, Jacob jr   335
Easter, Thomas   76, 80, 119, 360, 500
Eborn,   931, 932
Eborn, Henry   7, 35, 46, 53, 64, 116, 146, 268
Eborn, Jaccums   361
Eborn, James   10, 54, 86, 146, 268, 393, 403, 489, 927
Eborn, Joakim   255
Eborn, John   64, 69, 203, 512, 519, 907, 924
Eborn, Littleton   398
Eborn (Eborne), William   46, 53, 116
Eborn, William jr   145
Eborn, William sr   146
Eborn, Zenos   225
Eckols (Eckol), Joses (Joseph)   411, 435, 437
Egleton, John   4, 45, 79, 112, 347, 349, 352, 372, 428, 429
Egleton, Noah   334, 372
Elliot,   475
Ellison,   627
Elsbre, Ephraim   366, 374, 410, 423, 433, 434
English, James   186, 493
English, Joseph   447

English, Thomas   488
Ensley, John   49, 151
Ester, William   316, 935
Faddrey, John   941
Far, John   400
Farrow, Hezekiah   509
Farrow, John   508
Flinn (Flin),   6, 274
Flinn (Flin), Benjamin   3, 27, 195, 214
Flinn, Columb.   394
Flinn (Flin), Enoch   234, 252, 253, 356
Fodree, John   140
Fodrey,   309
Foreman,   485
Foreman, Alexander   139
Foreman, Benjamin   624, 906, 907
Foreman (Foriman, Foromam), Caleb   63, 231, 526
Foreman, Fredrick   512
Foreman, Joshua   11, 231
Foreman, Lazarus   106, 129, 526
Fortescue,   245
Fortescue, James   370
Fortescue, John jr   87
Fortescue, John sr   436
Fortescue, Samuel   436
Fortescue (Fortiscue), Seth   237, 429, 504, 526
Fortescue (Fortscue), William   82, 459
Fortiscue, Simon   84
Fortsine, John   77
Fortsyne, Bell   25
Fortsyne, Simon   26
Galard,   322
Galard, Thoms   325
Galberry,   30, 159
Gallaway (Gallowey), Abraham   109, 111, 314
Gallaway, Francis   110
Gallow, Abram   200
Galloway,   258

Gaylard, Benjamin   3, 167,
    252, 258, 477
Gaylard, Jeremiah   19, 20, 272
Gaylard (Gaylord), John   8,
    159, 372, 406
Gaylard (Galard, Gaylord),
    Stephen   3, 5, 6, 68, 252,
    256, 311, 477, 522
Gaylard, Thomas   1, 2, 6, 68,
    134, 282, 349, 372, 378,
    397, 406
Gaylard, Winfeild   68, 110
Gaylord,   38
Gaylord, James   73
Geben,   236
Germain, Henry   427
Gibbs,   49, 467, 479, 482,
    515
Gibbs, Benjamin   925
Gibbs, Benjamin jr   513
Gibbs, Benjamin sr   285
Gibbs, Cason   539, 540
Gibbs, John   467, 932
Gibbs, Thomas   187, 462
Gibbs, Thomas jr   513
Gibbs, Thomas sr   458
Gills,   475
Green, David (D)   47, 161,
    186, 244, 469, 924, 936,
    937, 942
Gurganes, Elious   273
Gurganis, Aron   248
Gurganis, Eleons   171
Gurganis, Samuel   248
Gurganus (Garganus,
    Gerganous, Gurganas),
    Jonathan   1, 2, 21, 42,
    406
Gurganus, Joseph   1
Gurganus, Samuel   134
Gurganus (Genganas), Wm
    363, 465
Hall,   132
Hall, James   505, 528
Hallon, Daniel   21
Hamilton,   245

Hamilton (Hambleton), James
    26, 82, 87, 88, 139, 247,

    276, 336, 341, 370, 412
Hamilton, John   25
Hammond, Boaz   139, 435
Hancock (Handcock),   309,
    486, 942
Hancock, Edward   1
Hancock, John   171
Hancock (Handcock), Joseph
    37, 85, 88, 152
Harris, Ezekiel   514
Harris, Ezekiel sr   542
Harris, Isaiah   515, 542
Harris, Peter   512
Harris, William   63, 482, 626,
    700, 912
Harris, William sr   467
Harvey,   209
Harvey, John   170
Harvey, John M   78, 537
Harvey, Nathan   238
Harvey (Havey), Richard   56,
    111, 121, 178, 200, 269,
    321, 322, 420, 523, 525,
    534, 909
Harvey, Richard jr   314, 543
Harvey, Richard sr   542
Henry, Hugh   482
Henry, Samuel   187, 516
Hernton, James   933
Hetherington, Charles   156
Hodges, James   480
Hodges, Robert   100
Hollon, Daniel   159, 171
Hollow,   209
Hollowell,   143, 931
Hollowell, Arthur   209
Hollowell, Benjamin   7, 35,
    37, 88, 166, 171, 255, 268,
    498
Hollowell, Joseph   114, 236
Hollowell, William   1, 35, 36,
    114, 133, 236, 268, 361, 527
Holms,   437

# Index to Hyde County, NC Land Entries


Holms, Archable   362
Homesley, Archable   410
Horth,   907
Hover, Seth   92
Hovey, Seth   170, 362, 410
Howard, William   357, 465, 472, 485
Howard, William sr   490
Huches,   495
Hudley,   12
Hunt, John   700
Hussey, Henry   131
Hussey, Mary   131
Hutson,   922
Hutson, Abel   459, 510
Jaccum,   361
Jackson, Eleaser   156
Jarot, Richard   130
Jarvis, David   942
Jarvis, Foster   510, 920, 921
Jarvis, Foster jr   918
Jarvis, James   921
Jarvis (Jarves, Jervis), Josiah   241, 242, 351, 428, 447, 473, 481, 918-921, 938, 940
Jarvis, Zachariah (Z)   487, 913, 921, 942
Jasper, James   323, 414, 416, 419
Jasper, Jonathan   419, 914
Jasper, Selden   323
Jasper, Valentine (Valinetine, Vallentine)   80, 119, 414, 416
Jasper, Willm J   344
Jenet, Robert   187
Jennet,   150
Jester, Ebenezer   470
Johnson (Johnston), Jeremiah (Jerimiah)   40, 57, 191, 194, 337, 409
Jolly, Philip   138
Jones,   6, 68, 81, 111, 121, 135, 236, 266, 267, 491, 912
Jones, Abraham (Abram)   40, 98, 161, 519
Jones, Abraham jr   40
Jones, Christopher   124, 165
Jones, James   28-30, 103, 104
Jones, Janus   532
Jones, Josiah   471
Jones, Roger   52, 454
Jones, Solomon   102, 470
Jones, Thomas   9, 41, 83, 206
Jordan,   132, 907, 926
Jordan, Abram   413
Jordan, James   450
Jordan, John   162, 164, 262, 316, 332, 395
Jordan, John sr   461
Jordan, Richard   250, 371
Jordan, Senhler   624
Jordan, Thomas   12, 163, 165, 168, 169, 173, 180, 341, 347, 413
Juell, Ebenezor   391
Juley, Jeremiah   48
Keach (Keech), Jasper   62, 65, 535
Keach, Joseph   624
Keech, James   64
Kirkonell, John   224
Lacey (Lacy), Parker   317, 339, 345, 346
Langly,   88
Larey, Simon   342
Lary, Salathul   494
Latham, Bartha   24
Latham, Jesse   353, 449, 502
Latham, Phineas (Phanius, Phinneis)   27, 36, 198, 274
Latham (Lotham), Rotheas (Bothas, Rothan, Rotheous)   27, 37, 75, 109, 195, 198, 208, 209, 443, 531
Layd,   1
Leach, Col.   200, 479
Leach (Leech), Joseph   114, 133, 259, 260, 310-313, 432
Leach, Joshua   261
Leath,   492
Leath, Charles   248

Leath, Saml   250, 275
Leech,           925
Lemount,           209
Letham, Chir   195
Levenworth, Henry   377
Lewis, John   322
Loyd, John   75, 112, 166, 203,
    280, 324, 349, 372
Loyhad, John   372
Mackduel, Sam   255
Mallison, John   503
Mallison (Malison), Thomas
    243, 503, 504
Mandowell, Samuel   59
Mandrick, John   366
Manduel,           257, 279
Manduel, Samuel   484
Martin,           324, 907
Martin, Benjamin   36, 42, 63,
    109, 198, 203, 356, 366,
    375, 442, 443
Martin, Daniel   106, 107
Martin, Hosea (Hose, Hosey)
    15, 22, 123, 195, 199, 442
Martin, Joel   86
Martin, Lovick   132
Mason,           162, 165, 922
Mason, Benjamin   99, 365,
    487, 920
Mason, Christopher   211, 306,
    339
Mason, James   517
Mason, John   224, 228, 529
Mason, Morris   211
Mason, Roger   913
Mason, Samuel   211, 935
Mason, Thomas   510, 529,
    913, 930, 935
Matthews, George   700-704
McCabe (McAbe), James   60,
    61, 66, 192, 338
McCabe, William   74
McCartey, Bailey   70
McCarty,           358, 359, 941
McCarty (McCorty), Archibald
    (Archabel)   500, 507, 933

McCarty, Darby   114
McSwain, Edward   203, 204,
    235, 279A, 281, 307, 324,
    325, 377
McWilliams,           246
McWilliams, Peter   30, 33
McWilliams (Mack Williams),
    Thos   264, 265, 420, 446
Mecarty, D   524
Meeatry,           140
Meline,           325
Mickins, James   396
Mixon, William   6
Molesley, Edward   362
Molin, Robert   235
Moline,           282
Mollerson, John   411
Moor, William   63, 138
Moorey, Timothy   41
Mordick (Mordrick),           144,
    429
Mordick, Benjamin   106, 107
Mordick (Mordrick), John
    106, 107, 362
Mordick, Levi   156
Morris, Elisha   142
Morris (Morriss), Francis   44,
    55, 340, 342
Mosley,           410
Murphy,           463
Nash,           202, 329
Nash, Thomas   113
Nehell, Valentine   251
Nole, Chinkepine   378
North,           158
Pain,           932
Pairtree, Holms (Holems)   435,
    452
Palmer,           136, 348
Palmer, Len   511
Palmer, Richard   313
Palmer, Robert   81, 127
Palmer, William   101, 224,
    515
Pampli,           238
Parker, Thomas   309

Parmelee, Benjamin   451
Parmer,   926
Paul, Jacob   28, 31, 67, 122, 189, 190, 205, 409, 536
Perkins, David   441
Petres,   479
Philips, John   334
Phillips (Philips), Jonathan   38, 114
Picquet (Picquit), Joseph   471, 473, 936
Ploint,   942
Poole (Pool), John   25, 141
Pormer, Robert   912
Porter,   502, 533
Porter, William   95
Porter, William jr   541
Potter, John   26
Price,   85
Price, William   7, 37, 171
Proctor,   935
Proctor, John   930
Purchase, Willm   341
Purkins,   86, 115
Pyott, William   537
Ray,   122
Rees, John   360
Rew, Fredrick   506
Rew, John   25, 26, 48
Rew, Mark   25, 70, 506
Rew, Solomon   317, 339, 500
Rew, Southy (Sauthey, Sothey, Southey)   117, 229, 345, 346, 928, 942
Rew, Southy jr   317
Rigney, John   230
Robins, James   440
Rogers, Benjamin   206-208, 321, 448, 525
Rogers, Isaac   189
Russel (Russell), Benjaman   9, 18, 126, 136, 149, 364, 511, 905, 928, 929
Russel, W   913, 914
Russel (Russell), William   81, 99, 124, 127, 157, 158, 226,

326, 348, 365, 373, 388, 511, 905
Sadler, John   471, 473, 936, 937
Sage,   143
Sanders, Andrew   353, 455
Sanderson,   245, 340
Sanderson, Benjamin   43, 44
Sanderson, Richard   285
Satchwell, John   448
Satterthwaite,   432
Satterthwaite (Satterwhite), Abraham   271, 315
Satterthwaite (Saterthwait), Jonathan   121, 543
Satterthwaite (Sattarthwaite, Satterthwait), William   18, 32, 41, 83
Scott,   460
Scott, Henry   363, 453, 465, 484, 485
Scott, Henry jr   472, 484, 485, 490
Selby (Silby), Henry   502, 537, 594, 598
Selby (Sebby, Sibly), Nathan   102, 470, 936, 937
Selby (Seby, Silby), Samuel   456, 519, 936, 937
Serman, Peter   508
Silby,   480
Silby, Burage H   424, 442-444
Silven, John   363
Silverthorm,   25
Silvester,   136, 154, 226, 251, 277
Silvester, Elisabeth (Elizebeth, Elisa)   233, 239, 306, 371, 376
Simmons, Edward   498, 499
Simpson, Samuel   357
Sinclear,   13
Sinnon, Joseph   519
Sivindell,   93
Slade,   336, 349
Slade, Benjamin   76, 89

Slade (Slaide), Ebenezor   367
Slade, Enoch   76, 119
Slade, Henry   364, 367
Slade, Hezekiah   26, 360
Slade, John   391, 396, 468
Slade, Reuben (Ruben)   154,
   226, 394
Slade, Rolin   226
Slade, Samuel   33, 91, 436,
   439, 451, 524
Slade, Willm H   329, 929
Smith,         249, 922, 941
Smith, Charles   77, 373, 374,
   408, 496, 511, 521
Smith, Elizabeth   246
Smith, James   490
Smith, John   136, 149, 155,
   226, 327, 371, 625
Smith, John sr   513
Smith, Joseph   460, 483, 485
Smith, Joshua   17, 246, 420
Smith, Rd   446
Smith, Solomon (Solleman,
   Soloman)   15, 16, 22, 30,
   32, 90, 123, 142, 174-179,
   192, 194, 204, 428, 525,
   527
Smith, Stephen (Stephin)   17,
   113, 246, 318, 327-329, 333,
   420
Smith, Thomas   14, 373, 374,
   414, 416, 496, 511, 521
Smith, William   700-704
Spady, Peter   522, 523
Spain (Span), Augustin   160,
   240, 244, 447
Span, Alyaslus   471
Springs,         58
Stakesbouy, J P   931
Stedman, Benjamin   13
Stilley, Hezekiah (Ezekiah)
   337,   338, 544
Sullivan,         464
Swindell (Swindal),         94,
   479, 520, 925, 926
Swindell (Swindal, Swindell),

   Caleb   23, 94, 96, 153, 445
Swindell, Christopher   917,
   923
Swindell, Ezekiah   474
Swindell, Isaac   101
Swindell, Jacob   354, 474
Swindell (Swindel), John   101,
   232, 626
Swindell, Josiah   118, 495
Swindell (Swindel, Swindal),
   Zedekiah (Zedikiah)   118,
   308, 330, 354
Taley, John   459
Tarner, George   627
Thoreogeoas, Esther   503
Thoroughgood, Ragil   53
Thorrington (Thorington,
   Thorroton), William   95,
   152, 187
Tison, Mathias   130
Toley (Toly, Tuley),         163,
   164, 930
Tooley (Tuley), Anthony   120,
   316, 317, 332, 919, 928, 940
Tooley, Henry   476
Tooley, John   227, 228
Tooley (Tooly, Tuely, Tuley),
   Jeremiah   84, 227-229, 390
Tooly (Tuely, Tuley), Levy
   (Levi)   262, 316, 332, 390
Topping, Thomas   19, 159
Toreman, Benjamin   460
Toreman, Caleb   460
Troop, William   143
Tuely, Jacob   355
Tuley, Able   70
Tuley, Thaniel   316
Tuley, Thomas   919
Tuley, Thomas sr   497
Turley,         124
Turner, William   97, 108, 186,
   488
Tyson (Tycon), Daniel   263,
   414, 446
Tyson, John   183, 350
Tyson, Matthias (Mathias)   82,

416, 419
Tyson (Tycon), Rebecca   446
Tyson, Zacheriah   417
Wade,          357, 379
Watson, Israel   94, 96, 445,
   520, 911
Watson, James   96
Watson, William   23, 93, 94,
   96, 445, 456, 520, 627, 916
Watson, William sr   445, 911
Webster,          58
Webster, James   11, 413, 440
Webster, John   170, 197, 209
Webster (Websten), William
   197, 236
Wedkins, Lettelton   58
Weeks,          362
Weston,          456, 910, 915
Weston, Joseph   100
Weston, Samuel   462, 539, 923
Whetor, Caleb   538
White,          93
White, Caleb   147
Whright, Thomas   12
Wiley, Elizabeth   446
Wilkerson, Isaack   398, 407
Wilkerson, Jacob   397
Wilkerson, James   315, 318,
   319, 326, 328, 329, 333,
   430, 431
Wilkin,          209
Wilkins, Littleton   58, 92, 128
Wilkinson, Abraham sr   312
Wilkinson, Abram   181, 182,
   184, 185, 271
Wilkinson, Isaac   499
Wilkinson, Isrel   236
Wilkinson, Jacob   282
Wilkinson (Willikison), James
   183, 185, 202, 270, 271, 929
Wilkinson, John   205
Williams, Patrick   492
Williams, William   470
Winby, Moses sr   7
Windfield, John   110, 114, 133
Windfield, Robert   111

Windfield, William   135
Windley,          88
Windley (Windly), Church   52,
   392
Windley, John   45
Windley (Windly, Wirly),
   Maple (Mapel)   45, 52, 79,
   454
Windley, Michael (Mikell)
   393, 403
Windley (Windly, Winley),
   Moses   10, 54, 79, 115
Windley (Windly), Seth   52,
   79, 454, 463
Windly, Shadrack   472, 484
Winfield, James   174, 201
Winfield (Winfild), John   278,
   934
Winfield, John sr   426, 427
Winfield, Richard   934
Winfield, Robert   200, 314
Winn,          197
Winn (Win), William   143,
   263, 284, 329
Wood, John   463
Wright, John   402
Wright (Whright), Thos   12,
   450
Wright, William   401
Wright, Williams W   402

Geographical locations:
Bay, bluf   157
Bay, Deep   99
Bay, Hern   917, 923
Bay, Horon   509
Bay, Jacobs   355
Bay, Juniper   97, 105, 108,
   160, 161, 186, 242, 298,
   303, 447, 481, 494, 924,
   938, 939
Bay, Mason   344, 390
Bay, Pains   932
Bay, Price   455
Bay, Prince   353
Bay, Rose   344, 497, 529

Bay, Rows   162, 196, 304, 305
Bay, Southwest   494, 540
Bay, Swan [Swam] Quarter
    140, 141, 152, 155, 241,
    249, 295, 296, 299, 309,
    467, 468, 471, 473, 481,
    487, 510, 625, 913, 918-922,
    936-942
Bay, patent   261, 432
Bay, the   228
Bluff, Pungo (Machpongo)
    102, 157, 188
Branch, Ash   446
Branch, Canoe   446
Branch, great   34, 50, 74
Branch, Juniper   351, 532
Branch, Mill   6
Branch, Ozbens   20
Branch, Savannah   59
Branch, Turkey (Turky)   65,
    624
Bridge, Indian Run   125
Bridge, old   401
Bridge, the   392
Canal, the   251
Causeway (Cosway), Great
    Swamp   200
Cod, Deep   53
Cove, Rush point   390
Coves, the   514
Creek, Arthurs   199
Creek, Ash   87, 276, 387
Creek, Back   357, 368
Creek, Berrey's   150
Creek, Brites (Brights)   444
Creek, Broad   2, 7, 8, 14, 19,
    21, 35, 37, 59, 85, 88, 159,
    255, 268, 279, 290, 293,
    350, 361, 390, 397, 408, 914
Creek, C. Smith   77
Creek, Capps   470
Creek, Cedar (Seder)   44, 55,
    77, 340
Creek, Collins   417
Creek, Counning Harbour   120
Creek, Cupton's   430

Creek, Deep   25, 935
Creek, Depps   202
Creek, Dips   329, 929
Creek, Dowry (Dowrey)   135,
    259, 260, 491
Creek, Ducking   87, 89, 391
Creek, Dunkin   387
Creek, Edmons   82
Creek, Fork   226
Creek, Fortscue   48
Creek, Holidays   129
Creek, Hudley's   12
Creek, Indian   84
Creek, Ingoes   407
Creek, Jacks   418
Creek, Jarves'   212
Creek, Jaspers   345, 346, 368
Creek, Joes   367
Creek, Jones   259, 260, 267,
    278, 628
Creek, Jordans   132
Creek, Juniper   102, 244, 488
Creek, King Georges   80
Creek, Lightwood   98
Creek, Little Olter   343
Creek, Long   368
Creek, Midle   49
Creek, N Dividing   129, 138,
    139, 144, 156, 237, 238,
    243, 405, 411, 421, 425,
    433, 434, 452, 504
Creek, Noans   488
Creek, Nocking Hammock
    228, 229
Creek, Northwest   160
Creek, Old Mattamuskeet   49
Creek, Olter   343
Creek, Otter   354
Creek, Oyster (Oeshter)   241,
    249, 401, 913, 921
Creek, Oyster shel   230, 245,
    276
Creek, Pantego (Pontegoe,
    Pantigo)   5, 6,   27, 36, 68,
    110, 112, 145, 195, 198,
    234, 236, 253, 274, 279A,

# Index to Hyde County, NC Land Entries


281, 307, 311, 335, 349,
366, 372, 375, 377, 394,
398, 406, 407
Creek, Pontegon   3
Creek, Prices   13
Creek, Pungo   10, 46, 52, 53,
63, 77, 86, 116, 363, 392,
393, 424, 441, 460, 464,
465, 473, 483-485, 489, 490,
512, 535, 603, 906, 931
Creek, Rattlesnake   242
Creek, Rusmans   315, 319
Creek, Rutneys   181
Creek, Severn   235
Creek, Shallop   439
Creek, Shallow   71
Creek, Sheds   44, 77
Creek, Silvester's (Sylvesters)
136, 154, 369, 373, 374,
376, 496
Creek, Slades   87, 89, 247,
276, 323, 340, 364, 367,
387, 389, 391, 412, 414-417,
419, 436, 451, 908, 933
Creek, Slake   245
Creek, Sluds   82
Creek, Smiths   81, 348, 371,
408,
496
Creek, Tysons   417, 419
Creek, Uper Island   390
Creek, Upper Dowry   934
Creek,   Wapoping   (Wappaping)
187, 513, 516
Creek, Well   938
Creek, Will   447
Creek, Woodstock   170,
180-182, 184
Creek, Writes   399
Creek, Wyesocking
(Wysoching, Waseoking,
Wesockin)   78, 98, 537,
594, 598
Dismal, Back   4, 38, 454
Ditch, the   89
Elbow, place   448

Flats, lake   251
Flats, Mattamuskeet Lake   528,
542
Flatts, the   515
Folly, D. Davis'   155
Glade, little   11
Glade, the   55, 76
Glen, Ezekiel   188
Ground, ready   931
Grove, Poyney   56
Gut, Holloways   237
Gut, small   89, 443
Gut, the   76, 129
Gutt, Grass Ridge   423
Gutt, J. Far's   400
Hills, Sand   353, 455, 932
Indian, line   224, 285
Indians, Mattamuskeet   251
Island, Judas   476
Island, Keepers   522
Knoll, oak   125
Knoll, small   463
Knolls, White Oak   126
Lake, Elbo   24
Lake, Mattamuskeet   23, 47,
78, 93-96, 100, 101, 118,
147, 153, 172, 196, 215-223,
251, 254, 285, 295-299, 302,
304, 305, 308, 330, 354,
456, 457, 461, 462, 466,
474, 475, 478-480, 482, 493,
495, 502, 505, 514, 515,
517-520, 528, 533, 537-539,
541, 542, 594, 626, 627,
629, 700, 910-912, 915-917,
923-926
Lake, old   160
Lake, Pungo (Pongo)   177
Lake, the   224, 303, 445, 473
Land, new   232
Landing, Bishop's   34
Landing, Dikes'   327
Landing, Logd house   310
Landing, old   177
Landing, Old shop   399
Landing, the   50

Landing, White Ouck   60
Loul, Hickary   125
MD, Baltimore   700-704
Marsh, the   12, 76, 113, 129, 329
Marshes, Bluf   157
Marshes, Narrow   99
Marshes, Pungo Bluf   157
Marshes, Swan Island   227
Martin, patent   324
Mills, Broad Creek   288
NC, Bath   170
NC, Beaufort Co   4
NC, Currituck Co   509, 524
NC, New Currituck twsp.   25, 26, 48, 70, 80, 81, 84, 163-165, 172, 211, 215-223, 227, 228, 239, 245, 254, 297, 302, 316, 339, 345, 346, 348, 358-360, 365, 368, 371, 387, 391, 500, 506, 928, 930, 935
NC, Tyrrell Co   322
NC, Woodstock   310
Neck, Jacks   236, 394, 427
Neck, Tarkiln   173
Neck, Turkey   268
Oak, hiding   503
Office, T. Jordan's Entry   341
Pasture, Holms   437
Pasture, P. Lacy's   346
Pasture, S. Rew's   345
Pier, J. Aldorson's   908
Pleasant, Mount   508
Pocosin, Back   5, 9, 41, 225
Pocosin, Hack   134
Pocosin, the   27, 45, 92, 213, 329, 497, 529
Point, Island   390
Point, Juells   76
Point, Lookout   327
Point, Piney   210
Point, Sandy   44
Point, Swearing (Swaring)   17, 310
Point, the   353

Point, Wades   357, 379
Point, Wappoping   150, 151
Point, Well   939
Pond (Pound), Mill   375
Pond, Pantigo Mill   356, 498, 499
Pond, Z. Eborn's mill   225
Quay, J. Aldorson's   908
Reeds, Bed of   530
Reeds, Great bend of   15
Ride, Langly's   88
Ridge, Arnols   71
Ridge, Beach (Beech)   114, 259, 260, 263, 264, 278, 427
Ridge, Chinkopin   242
Ridge, G. Duke   73
Ridge, Grapevine   9
Ridge, Grassey   66, 338, 423
Ridge, Great   388, 905
Ridge, Holly (Holley)   63, 454
Ridge, Hooppool   52
Ridge, Moses   9
Ridge, Mulberry (Malberry, Mulbrey)   78, 537, 594, 598
Ridge, Northeast   90
Ridge, Oack   61, 72
Ridge, Paupau   365
Ridge, Pine Grove   909
Ridge, Poiney   72
Ridge, Post oak   241, 939
Ridge, Prices   4
Ridge, Rays   122
Ridge, the   923
Ridges, Chinkcopine   137
Ridges, Oak   105
Ridges, Stamping   523
River, Alligator   501
River, Long Shoal (Shold)   330, 353, 354, 455, 466, 474, 501, 518, 608, 609, 629, 932
River, main   206
River, Pamlico   347, 352, 357, 379, 400, 433, 435, 437, 452
River, Pungo (Machapungo, Pongo)   3, 6, 8, 9, 18, 24,

32, 34, 38, 39, 41, 44,
55-58, 60, 61, 66-68,
72-74, 76, 85-92, 103, 104,
106, 107, 111, 113, 114,
117, 119, 121-137, 142-144,
146, 148, 149, 154, 158,
167, 174-176, 178, 179,
183, 185, 192, 195, 199,
201, 204, 205, 208, 225,
226, 231, 233, 245-248, 250,
256-258, 261, 263, 266, 267,
269-271, 275, 283, 306,
307, 310, 311, 314, 315,
318-323, 326-329, 331,
335-338, 340, 350, 351, 357,
360, 369-371, 373, 376,
379-387, 389, 391, 393, 394,
396, 401-405, 408-410,
412-424, 426-433, 436,
438-440, 443, 444, 446,
448-451, 453, 459, 477, 491,
492, 496, 499, 511, 512,
522-525, 527, 530-532, 534,
536, 543-558, 604-607, 624,
908, 909, 914, 927-929, 931,
933
Road, Juniper Bay   924
Road, main   21, 446
Road, old   8
Road, the   13, 67, 161, 170
Run, Deep   27, 35, 36, 198,
268
Run, Ford   104, 125, 126
Run, Fork   57
Run, Heren   327
Run, Indian   40, 57, 104, 125,
126, 137, 174, 322, 409,
536, 544
Savannah, Lake   141
Savannah, Murphy's   463
Savannah, Piney   535
Savannah, Poiney   62, 64
Savannah, the   13, 47, 442,
473
Savannah, Windley's   88
Shipyard, J. Jasper's   419

Shore, river   43
Sound, Albemarle   705-741,
749-755, 767-805, 812-817,
849-852, 859-869, 871-873,
875-879, 886-904A
Sound, Pamlico   705-741,
749-755, 767-805, 812-817,
849-852, 859-869, 871-873,
875-879, 886-904A
Sound, the   932
Swamp, Back   3, 31, 34, 57,
189, 205, 207
Swamp, Back Dismal   454
Swamp, Broad Creek   19, 272,
273, 286-289, 291, 292, 294,
312, 378
Swamp, Currituck   124
Swamp, Cypress (cypress)   41,
327, 344, 351
Swamp, Enward   3
Swamp, Fork Run   57, 126
Swamp, Green   269
Swamp, Gum   166
Swamp, Indian Run   67, 194
Swamp, Juniper   501, 544
Swamp, Lake   22, 32
Swamp, Leaurel   168, 169
Swamp, Lorril   64
Swamp, Mattamuscat   150, 151
Swamp, Meeatry's   140
Swamp, Mill   290
Swamp, New Currituck   313,
317, 332, 511
Swamp, Pantego (Pantigo)   42,
75, 109, 166, 167, 203, 256,
280, 324, 334
Swamp, Piney   110, 121
Swamp, Point Lookout   327
Swamp, Pungo   4, 52, 54, 454
Swamp, Pungo Creek   603
Swamp, river   15, 16, 17, 24,
28, 29, 30, 31, 34, 40, 50,
51, 56, 57, 60, 66
Swamp, river   83, 327, 525
Swamp, Woodstock Creek   312
Woods, High   229

Woodyard, Savannah Devil
  410

www.ingramcontent.com/pod-product-compliance
Lightning Source LLC
Chambersburg PA
CBHW022112050726
47591CB00002B/771